Holy Vedas

Wisdom from the Sacred Teachings of Hinduism

Swami Divyananda

Hindu Philosophy Council

GRAPEVINE INDIA

Published by

GRAPEVINE INDIA PUBLISHERS PVT LTD

www.grapevineindia.com
Delhi | Mumbai
email: grapevineindiapublishers@gmail.com

Ordering Information:
Quantity sales: Special discounts are available on quantity purchases by corporations, associations, and others.
For details, reach out to the publisher.

First published by Grapevine India 2023

CONTENTS

RIG VEDA

CREATION

I. HYMN OF CREATION

X, 129. METRE: TRISTUBH.

1. Non-being then existed not nor being:
There was no air, nor sky that is beyond it.
What was concealed? Wherein? In whose protection?
And was there deep unfathomable water?

2. Death then existed not nor life immortal;
Of neither night nor day was any token.
By its inherent force the One breathed windless:
No other thing than that beyond existed.

3. Darkness there was at first by darkness hidden;
Without distinctive marks, this all was water.
That which, becoming, by the void was covered,
That One by force of heat came into being.

4. Desire entered the One in the beginning:
It was the earliest seed, of thought the product.
The sages searching in their hearts with wisdom,
Found out the bond of being in non-being.

5. Their ray extended light across the darkness:
But was the One above or was it under?
Creative force was there, and fertile power:
Below was energy, above was impulse.

6. Who knows for certain? Who shall here declare it?
Whence was it born, and whence came this creation?
The gods were born after this world's creation:
Then who can know from whence it has arisen?

7. None knoweth whence creation has arisen;
And whether he has or has. not produced it;
He who surveys it in the highest heaven,
He only knows, or haply he may know not.

VARUNA

The greatest of the gods of the Rigveda, beside Indra, is Varuna, though the number of hymns in which he alone (apart from Mitra) is addressed is only 12, as compared with the 250 to Indra. His physical features and activities are mentioned: he has face, eye, arms, hands and feet; he walks, drives, sits, eats and drinks. His eye, with which he observes mankind, is the sun. He sits on the strewn grass at the sacrifice. He wears a golden mantle or a shining robe. His car, drawn by well-yoked steeds, gleams like the sun. Varuna sits in his mansion surveying the deeds of men; and the Fathers behold him in the highest heaven. He has spies who sit around him and observe the two worlds. By his golden- winged messenger the sun is meant. He is often called a king, but especially a universal monarch. His sovereignty, his divine dominion, and his occult power (mayo) are specially emphasized. Varuna is characteristically an upholder of physical and moral order, the great maintainer of the laws of nature. He established heaven and earth, which he keeps asunder. He caused the sun to shine in heaven, and made for it a wide path. He placed fire in the waters and Soma on the rock. The wind that resounds through the air is his breath. By his ordinance the moon shining brightly moves at night, and the stars disappear by day. He is thus lord of light, both by day and by night. Varuna is also a regulator of the waters: he made the rivers flow; by his occult power they pour swiftly into the ocean without filling it. He is, however, more frequently connected with the atmospheric waters: thus he causes the inverted cask (the cloud) to shed its waters on heaven, earth and air, and to moisten the ground.

The fixity of his laws, which the gods themselves follow, is frequently mentioned. His power is so great that neither the birds as they fly, nor the rivers as they flow, can reach the limits of his dominion, His omniscience is typical: he knows the flight of the birds in the sky, the path of the ships in the ocean, the course of the far-travelling wind; he beholds all the secret things that have been or shall be done, and witnesses men's truth and falsehood; no creature can even wink without his knowledge.

Varuna is pre-eminent among the Vedic gods as a moral ruler. His anger is aroused by sin, which he severely punishes. The fetters with which he binds sinners are characteristic of him. But he is merciful to the penitent, releasing them from sin, even that committed by their fathers, and from guilt due to thoughtlessness. Every hymn addressed to Varuna contains a prayer for forgiveness of sin. Varuna is on a footing of friendship with his worshipper, who communes with him in his heavenly mansion, and sometimes sees him with his mental eye. The righteous hope to behold in the next world Varuna and Yama (the god of Death), the two kings who reign together in bliss.

Varuna seems originally to have represented the encompassing sky. But this conception has become obscured in the Rigveda, because it dates from a pre-

Vedic period. It goes back to the Indo-Iranian age at least; for the Ahura Mazda, the "wise spirit" of the Avesta, agrees closely with the Asura (divine spirit) Varuna in character, though not in name. It may be even older, as Varuna is perhaps identical with the Greek oupavo "sky." At any rate, the name appears to be derived from the root vr, to "cover" or "encompass."

VII, 88. MKTRE: TRISTUBH.

1. Present to Varuna the gracious giver
A hymn, Vasistha, bright and very pleasant,
That he may bring to us the lofty, holy
And mighty steed that grants a thousand bounties.

2. Now having come to Varuna's full aspect,
I think his countenance like that of Agni;
May he, the lord, lead me to see the marvel:
The light and darkness hidden in the cavern.

3. When Varuna and I the boat have mounted
And have propelled it to the midst of ocean;
When we shall move across the waters' ridges
We'll waver in the swing to raise its lustre.

4. Varuna has placed Vasistha in the vessel;
The sage benignant by his mighty power
His praiser in prosperity has settled,
As long as days endure, as long as mornings.

5. What has become of those our former friendships,

When we two held erstwhile unbroken converse?

O sovereign Varuna, thy lofty mansion,

Thy home, I entered, with its thousand portals.

6. Who is, O Varuna, thy constant kinsman,

Once dear, though sinful now, he claims thy friendships.

As guilty may we not, O wizard, suffer:

Do thou, O sage, grant shelter to thy praiser.

7. O may we, in these fixed abodes abiding,

Now from the lap of Aditi find favour.

May from his noose king Varuna release us.

Ye gods protect us evermore with blessings.

MITRA

Mitra is so intimately associated with Varuna that he is invoked alone in only one hymn of the Rigveda. The information about him in his separate capacity being so limited, his individual character is somewhat indefinite. He is the great Aditya who by his voice marshals men and watches the tillers with unwinking eye. That he is thought of as regulating the course of the sun is indicated by the fact that the solar deity Savitar is identified with him because of his laws, and another solar deity, Visnu, takes his three strides by the laws of Mitra. Agni, who is kindled before dawn, is said to produce Mitra, and when kindled is identified with Mitra. In the Atharvaveda Mitra at^sunrise is contrasted with Varuna in the evening, and in the Brahmanas Mitra is associated with day, Varuna with night.

The Vedic evidence thus indicates that Mitra is a solar deity. This conclusion is confirmed by the cognate Iranian religion, in which Mithra is undoubtedly a sun-god. The kindly nature of Mitra is often referred to in the Veda; the word also frequently means "friend" in the Rigveda, and in the Avesta Mithra is the guardian of faithfulness. The inference thus is that mitra, friend, was originally a term applied to the sun-god in his capacity of a beneficent power of nature.

III, 59. METRE: 1-5 TRISTUBH ; 6-9 GAYATRI.

1. Mitra stirs men to action when he calls them;

Mitra supported both the Earth and Heaven;

Mitra with steady eye regards the people:

To Mitra offer now with ghee oblation.

2. Let him who, Mitra L brings thee food be foremost,

Who to thy law, O Aditya, pays homage.

Aided by thee no man is slain or vanquished;

To him from near or far no trouble reaches.

3. Free from disease, in sacred food delighting,

With knees set firm upon the earth's wide surface.

In this Aditya's sacred law abiding,

May we remain in the good will of Mitra.

4. This Mitra, worshipped and most propitious,

Is born to wield fair sway, a king, disposer.

May we rest in the grace of him the holy,

May we abide in his most kindly favour.'

5. The great Aditya to be served with homage,

Who stirs mankind, to singers most propitious:

To him most highly to be praised, to Mitra,

In fire present acceptable oblations.

6. The grace of Mitra, the divine

Supporter of mankind, brings gain

And splendour with most brilliant fame.

7. Mitra, whose fame is spread abroad,

In greatness who transcends the sky,

And in renown transcends the earth.

8. The peoples five submission yield

To Mitra ever strong to aid:

'Tis he who all the gods sustains.

9. Mitra, among both gods and men,

For him who strews the sacred grass

Has furnished food fixed by his will.

MITRA AND VARUNA

These two gods are addressed as a pair in the dual more frequently than any other couple except Heaven and Earth. The hymns in which they are thus conjointly invoked are far more numerous than those in which they are separately addressed. As Mitra by himself has hardly any individual traits, the two gods together have practically the same attributes and functions as Varuna (p. 20) alone.

Mitra-Varuna are young and wear glistening garments. Their eye is the sun; they drive with the rays of the sun as with arms. They mount their car in the highest heaven. Their abode, which is golden, is located in heaven; it is great, very lofty, firm, with a thousand pillars and a thousand doors. They have spies who are wise and cannot be deceived. They are kings and universal monarchs, rulers and guardians of the whole world, who support heaven, air and earth. They are also called "divine spirits" (asura), who wield dominion by means of occult power. By that power they send the dawns, make the sun traverse the sky, and obscure it with cloud and rain. They are lords of rivers, and they are the gods most frequently thought of and prayed to as bestowers of rain. One entire hymn dwells on their powers of granting rain. They control the rainy skies and the streaming waters. They send rain and refreshment from the sky. They bedew the pastures with ghee (i.e. rain) and the spaces with honey. Mitra-Varuna are upholders and cherishers of order (rta). Their ordinances are fixed and cannot be in- fringed even by the immortal gods. They are barriers against falsehood, which they dispel, hate, and punish. They afflict with disease those who neglect their worship. The dual worship of this divine pair goes back to the Indo-Iranian period, as Ahura and Mithra are thus coupled in the Avesta.

IV. MITRA AND VARUNA

VII, 61. METRE : TRISTUBH.

1. The beauteous eye of Varuna and Mitra,

The Sun, now rises up, his light extending,

Who with his gaze looks down upon all creatures:

He ever notes the burning zeal of mortals.

2. This pious priest, heard far away, here utters

His hymn for you, O Varuna and Mitra:
Do ye, O sages, treat his prayers with favour,
And may his autumns be replete with wisdom.

3. From wide-spread earth, O Varuna and Mitra,
Ye bounteous gods, and from the lofty heaven,
Ye have disposed your wander ing spies in dwellings
And plants, ye who with watchful eye protect us.

4. Praise thou the law of Varuna and Mitra:
Their force the two worlds keeps with might asunder.
The months of impious men shall pass by sonless;
May those on worship bent increase their homestead.

5. Ye both are wise, O mighty ones, for you two
These lauds are sung without deceit or magic.
Avenging spies pursue men's falsehoods closely:
There are no secrets that ye cannot fathom.

6. With reverence I will consecrate your offering;
With zeal I call you, Varuna and Mitra.
These novel thoughts to praise you are intended:
May these the prayers that I have offered please you.

7. For you, O gods, this service has been rendered
At sacrifices, Varuna and Mitra.
Across all dangers do ye safely take us.
Ye gods protect us evermore with blessings.

THE ADITYAS

The group of gods called Adityas is celebrated in six entire hymns of the Rigveda and in parts of two others. Their original number was seven, but in one passage of the last book, an eighth, Martanda (probably the setting sun) is added. In the Atharvaveda their number is eight. In the Brahmanas it has grown to twelve ; and in post-Vedic literature these are regularly twelve sun-gods connected with the twelve months. The names of the gods included in this group are not quite definite. Nowhere are more than six enumerated, and that only once: Mitra, Aryaman, Bhaga, Varuna, Daksa, Amsa. In a few passages Surya is called an Aditya, which is a common name of the sun in the Brahmanas and later. He is therefore probably to be regarded as the seventh Aditya. Indra is, however, once coupled_in the dual as an Aditya with Varuna, the chief of the Adityas, and he is once directly invoked as the "fourth Aditya." When mention is made of one Aditya, it is generally Varuna; when of two, Mitra and Varuna; when of three, Varuna, Mitra, and Aryaman; when of five (which is only once the case}, Varuna, Mitra, Aryaman, Bhaga, and Savitar. The Adityas are often invoked as a group, when the names of Mitra and Varuna are generally mentioned at the same time. The nature of the Adityas as a class resembles that of the gods in general. In the aggregate sense they are the gods of celestial light, without representing any particular manifestation of that light. In some of the hymns in which the Adityas are invoked, only the three most frequently mentioned together Mitra, Varuna and Aryaman seem to be meant. The name of the Adityas is a metronymic formation from that of their mother, Aditi, with whom they are naturally often invoked.

v. ADITYAS

II, 27. METRE: TRISTUBH.

1. These songs that drip with butter, with the ladle

I ever to the kings, Adityas, offer.

May Mitra, Aryaman, and Bhaga hear us,

Daksa, the mighty Varuna, and Amsa.

2. This praise of mine may Aryaman and Mitra

And Varuna to-day accept united:

The radiant Adityas, like sword-blades shining,

From guile and falsehood free, unscathed, and blameless.

3. These Adityas are deep and far-extending,
With many eyes, deceived not, but deceiving.
They look within, and see the straight and crooked.
Nigh to the kings is all, even what is farthest.

4. The Adityas support what's fixed and moving;
These gods are guardians of the whole creation:
Far-sighted, cherishing their spirit-power,
Observing holy law and guilt chastising.

5. May I, O Adityas, meet with your favour,
Which even in danger, Aryaman, brings comfort.
Guided by you, O Varuna and Mitra,
May I avoid all troublous times, like pitfalls.

6. Smooth is your path, O Aryaman and Mitra;
It is straightforward, Varuna, and thornless.
On that, O Adityas, speak in our favour;
Bestow on us invincible protection.

7. May Aryaman, may Aditi, kings' mother,
By easy paths through enmities transport us.
We would unscathed, possessed of many heroes,
Win Varuna's and Mitra's high protection.

8. Three earths, three heavens, too, these gods supported,

Three are their services within our synod.
By Law is mighty, Adityas, your greatness
And fair, Aryaman, Varuna and Mitra.

9. Of golden aspect, radiant, bright, as sword-blades,
They have upheld the three light realms of heaven.
They slumber not, nor close their eyes, unfailing
They rule afar to help the truthful mortal.

10. Thou art, O Varuna, of all the sovereign,
Both of the gods, O Asura, and mortals.
To us vouchsafe to see a hundred autumns:
May we attain to lives prolonged and happy.

11. Neither the right nor left can I distinguish,
Neither before nor yet behind, Adityas.
May I by you directed, reach with safety,
Bright gods, the light by innocence or wisdom.

12. Who to the kings that lead the law pays worship,
And whom thus constant blessings cause to flourish,
He, affluent, rides foremost in his chariot,
Bestowing gifts and in assemblies lauded.

13. He pure, unhurt by guile, with many heroes,
Robust, abides by waters rich in pasture.
Either from near or from afar none slay him
Who lives beneath the Adityas' direction.

14. O Aditi and Varuna and Mitra,
Forgive us any sin we have committed.
May I obtain the light, secure and spacious,
O Indra ; may long darkness never reach us.

15. Both worlds, combined, for him shed in abundance
The rain of heaven; fortunate and thriving
He goes to battle, both the mansions winning.
For him the world's two halves remain propitious.

16. Your wiles, intended, holy gods, for plotters,
Your nooses, Adityas, for foes unloosened:
These would I pass, as with his car a driver;
May we unscathed be in your wide protection.

17. May I not ever lack a friendly patron,
Nor, Varuna, an open-handed comrade.
May I, O King, not want well-managed riches,
May we speak loud, with heroes, in the synod.

SURYA

Surya, who is addressed in about ten hymns of the Rigveda,) is the most concrete of the solar deities, because his name designates the orb of the sun as well as the god. The solar disc is often called the eye of Surya, or the eye of Mitra-Varuna, as well as of Agni and of the gods. He is all-seeing, the spy of the whole world, beholding the good and bad deeds of mortals. His car is drawn by a single steed or by seven swift mares. The Dawn reveals or produces Surya; like a lover he follows the radiant goddess. He arouses men to activity; he is the soul of all that moves or stands. He is the son of Heaven (Dyaus). Surya is variously described as a bird traversing space; as a mottled bull or a brilliant steed; as a gem of the sky, or a variegated stone set in the midst of heaven; as a brilliant weapon ; or as a wheel, though the wheel of Surya is also spoken of. He dispels the darkness, which he casts off like a skin. He measures the days and prolongs life. He drives away disease and evil dreams. All creatures depend on him, and he is "all-creating." At his rising he is implored to declare men sinless to Mitra-Varuna and to other gods.

I, 115. METRE: TRISTUBH.

1. The gods' refulgent countenance has risen,

The eye of Mitra, Varuna and Agni.

He has pervaded air, and earth, and heaven:

The soul of all that moves and stands is Surya.

2. The Sun pursues the Dawn, the gleaming goddess,

As a young man a maiden, to the region

Where god-devoted men lay on the harness

Of brilliant offerings for the brilliant godhead.

3. The brilliant steeds, bay coursers of the sun-god,

Refulgent, dappled, meet for joyful praises,

Wafting our worship, heaven's ridge have mounted,
And in one day round earth and sky they travel.

4. This is the Sun's divinity, his greatness:
In midst of action he withdraws the daylight.
When from their stand he has withdrawn his coursers,
Then straightway night for him spreads out her garment.

5. This form the Sun takes in the lap of heaven,
That Varuna and Mitra may regard him.
One glow of his appears unending, splendid;
His bay steeds roll the other up, the black one.

6. To-day, O gods, do ye at Surya's rising
Release us from distress and from dishonour:
This boon may Varuna and Mitra grant us,
And Aditi and Sindhu, Earth and Heaven.

I, 50. METRE : 1-9 GAYATRI ; 10 ANUSTUBH.

1. Aloft his beams now bring the god
Who knows all creatures that are born,
That all may look upon the Sun.

2. Away like thieves the stars depart,
By the dark nights accompanied,
At the all-seeing Sun's approach.

3. His beams, his rays, have shone afar
Athwart the many homes of men,
Flaming aloft like blazing fires.

4. Swift-moving, visible to all,
Maker of light thou art, O Sun,
Illuming all the shining space.

5. Thou risest toward the host of gods
And toward the race of men: toward all,
That they may see the heavenly light.

7. The broad air traversing, the sky,
Thou metest, Sun, the days with nights,
Seeing all creatures that are born,

8. The seven bay mares that draw thy car,
Bring thee to us, far-seeing god,
O Surya of the gleaming hair.

9. The Sun has yoked the seven bright mares,
The shining daughters of his car:
With that self-yoking team he speeds.

10. Athwart the darkness gazing up,
To him the higher light, we now
Have soared to Surya, the god
Among the gods, the highest light.

PUSAN

This god, who is celebrated in eight hymns, has a vague personality, with few anthropomorphic traits. His foot, his right hand, his beard and his braided hair are mentioned. He carries a golden spear, an awl and a goad. His car is drawn by goats instead of horses. Gruel is his characteristic food. He sees all creatures clearly. He moves onward, observing the universe, and makes his abode in heaven. He is a guardian who knows and surveys all creatures. He traverses the distant path of heaven and earth. With his golden aerial ships he acts as the messenger of Surya. As best of charioteers he drove down the golden wheel of the sun. He is the wooer of his mother and the lover of his sister (i.e. Dawn), and was given by the gods as a husband to the Sun-maiden, Surya. One of his exclusive epithets is "glowing." He conducts the dead on the far-off path of the Fathers. A guardian of roads, he removes dangers out of the way. He protects cattle, bringing them home when lost. The meaning of the name is "Prosperer." The evidence thus indicates that Pusan was originally a solar deity, chiefly as a benevolent patron of pastoral prosperity.

J, 42. METRE: GAYATRI,

J. O Pusan pass along the roads,

Free us, son of release, from care.

Guide us, going before, god,

2. The wicked, ill-intentioned wolf,

Pusan, that lies in wait for us,

Him from our path smite thou away.

3. The robber lurking round our path,

Who there against us mischief plots,

Far from the track drive him away.

4. Tread under foot the burning brand

Of crafty and malignant men,
The miscreants whoe'er they be.

5. Pusan, that help of thine we claim,
O wonder-working, sapient god,
Wherewith our fathers thou didst aid.

6. Thou, lord of all prosperity,
Best wielder of the golden axe,
Make easy wealth for us to gain.

7. Past our pursuers lead us, make
Fair paths, easy for us to tread.
Thus, Pusan, show in us thy might.

8. Lead us to pastures rich in grass,
Send on the road no early heat.
Thus, Pusan, show in us thy might.

10. We wrangle not with Pusan, him
We call upon with songs of praise:
For wealth we seek the wondrous god.

SAVITAR

Savitar is invoked in eleven whole hymns and in a good many detached stanzas as well. He is pre- eminently a golden deity. His golden car is drawn by two or more brown, white-footed steeds. With his golden arms, which he raises aloft, he arouses and blesses all beings. His mighty golden splendour illumines heaven, earth and air. He moves in his golden car on an upward and a downward path, observing all creatures. Yellow-haired, he constantly raises his light in the east. On his ancient paths in the air he conveys the dead to where the righteous dwell, He drives away evil dreams and sins, demons and sorcerers. He observes fixed laws. Wind and waters are subject to, and regulated by him. He brings not only day but night, when he sends all beings to rest. The other gods follow his lead, and no being can resist his will. To Savitar is addressed the most famous stanza of the Rigveda, which has been a morning prayer in India for more than 3,000 years. It is called the Savitri, from the name of the god invoked, or Gayatrl, from that of the metre in which it is composed: May we attain that excellent Glory of Savitar the God, that he may stimulate our thoughts.

Savitar is often distinguished from Surya, the sun. Thus he is said to shine with the rays of the sun, to impel the sun, or to declare men sinless to the sun The name is derived from the root su, "to stimulate," forms of which are perpetually used with it as an etymological play. The word deva," god," is constantly associated with his name, as with that of no other deity, in the sense of the "stimulator god." Savitar is thus a solar deity in the capacity of the great stimulator of life and activity in the world.

VI, 71. METRE : 1-3 JAGATI ; 5-6 TRISTUBH.

1. God Savitar, the dexterous, has stretched aloft

His arms, that he may stimulate all things to life.

Young, vigorous, most skilled, with fatness he

His hands besprinkles in the wide expanse of air.

2. May we possess god Savitar's most excellent

Impulsion, and enjoy his lavish gifts of wealth.

Thou art the god who sends to rest and wakes in turn

To life the whole two-footed and four-footed world.

3. With guards that never fail, auspicious, Savitar,
Protect our habitation all around to-day.
God of the golden tongue, for welfare ever new
Preserve us: let no plotter hold us in his grasp.

4. Like one who rouses, Savitar has stretched out
His golden arms that are so fair of aspect.
The heights of heaven and earth he has ascended,
And made each flying monster cease from troubling.

5. To-day wealth, Savitar, and wealth to-morrow,
Bring wealth to us each day by thine impulsion;
For over ample wealth, O god, thou rulest:
Through this our hymn may we of wealth be sharers.

VISNU

Visnu, though one of the two leading gods of modern Hinduism, is in the Rigveda as yet a minor deity, being addressed in only five or six hymns. The only anthropomorphic traits there attributed to him are that he is a youth of vast body and that he takes three strides. The latter is his chief characteristic, with which are associated his exclusive epithets of ' ' wide-going ' ' and ' ' wide- striding." With these steps he traverses the earth and the terrestrial regions. Two of his steps are visible to men, but the third is beyond the flight of birds or mortal ken. His highest step is like an eye fixed in heaven; it shines down brightly. Visnu's three strides undoubtedly refer to the course of the sun as it passes through the three divisions of the world: earth, air and heaven. Visnu is further said to set in motion his 90 steeds (i.e. days) with their four names (i.e. seasons), in allusion to the 360 days of the solar year. Thus Visnu seems to have been originally a personification of the sun in its activity of traversing the universe.

Visnu is described as taking his steps for man's existence, to bestow on him the earth as a dwelling place. The most prominent secondary characteristic of Visnu is his friendship with Indra, with whom he is often allied in his conflict with Vrtra. In hymns addressed to Visnu alone, Indra is the only other god incidentally associated with him. One hymn invokes these two gods conjointly.

I, 154. METRE: TRISTUBH.

1. I will proclaim the mighty deeds of Visnu,

Of him who measured out the earthly spaces:

Who, firmly propping up the higher station,

Strode out in triple regions, widely pacing.

2. Because of this his mighty deed is Visnu

Lauded, like some fierce beast that is much dreaded,

That wanders as it lists, that haunts the mountains:

He in whose three wide strides abide all creatures.

3. Let my inspiring hymn go forth to Visnu,
The mountain-dwelling bull, the widely pacing,
Him who has measured out with but three footsteps,
Alone, this long and far-extended station;

4. Him whose three footsteps filled with mead, unfailing,
Revel in blissful joy; who has supported
Alone the universe in three divisions:
The earth and sky and all created beings.

5. I would attain to that his dear dominion
Where men devoted to the gods do revel.
In the wide-striding Visnu's highest footstep
There is a spring of mead: such is our kinship.

6. We long to go to those your dwelling-places
Where are the kine with many horns, the nimble:
For thence, indeed, the highest step of Visnu,
Wide-pacing bull, shines brightly down upon us.

USAS

Usas, the goddess of Dawn, who is celebrated in some twenty hymns of the Rigveda, is but slightly personified, for the underlying physical phenomenon is never absent from the mind of the poet. She appears in the east, clothed in light, adorned with bright raiment like a dancer. She drives away the darkness and removes the black robe of night. Though ancient, she is ever young, being born again and again. She wastes away the life of mortals. She opens the gates of heaven, and her radiant beams appear like herds of cattle. She rides on a brilliant car, drawn by ruddy steeds or kine. She drives away bad dreams, evil spirits and the hateful darkness. When she shines forth, the birds fly from their nests, and men seek nourishment. She appears day after day at the appointed place, never infringing the law of nature and of the gods. She is born in the sky, and is constantly called the "daughter of heaven." She is also the elder sister of night, with whose name hers is often joined as a compound in the dual. She is closely associated with the Sun, who is her lover, following her as a young man a maiden. She thus often becomes the wife of Surya. But as preceding the sun, she is sometimes called his mother, and is thus said to arrive with a bright child. The sacrificial fire being lit at dawn, Usas is often associated with Agni, whom she causes to be kindled and who is sometimes called her lover. She is also often connected with the Asvins, the twin gods of early morning. As disclosing the treasures concealed by darkness, she distributes them liberally and is characteristically "bountiful." She not only brings the worshipper wealth and children, but bestows protection and long life, fame and glory on the benefactors of the poet.

Forms of the root vas, "to shine," from which the name of Usas is derived, are often used in describing her activity, somewhat in the same way as sil, "to stimulate," is used with the name of Savitar.

I, 92. METRE: 4 JAGATI; 5-12 TRISTUBH; 13-15 USNIH.

4. She throws gay garments round her like a dancing girl;

E'en as a cow her udder, she displays her breast.

Creating light for all the world, Dawn has unbarred

The gates of darkness as when cows break from their stall.

5. Her radiant shimmer has appeared before us;
It spreads, and drives away the swarthy monster.
As one anoints the post at sacrifices
The daughter of the sky extends her lustre.

6. We have crossed to the farther shore of darkness:
Dawn shining forth, her webs of light is weaving.
She smiles for glory, radiant, like a lover.
To show good will she, fair of face, has wakened.

7. The radiant leader of rich gifts, the daughter
Of Heaven by the Gotamas is lauded.
Mete out to us, O Dawn, largesses: offspring,
Brave men, conspicuous wealth in cows and horses.

8. May I attain that wealth renowned and ample,
With many heroes, troops of friends, and horses,
O Dawn, that shinest forth with wondrous glory,
Urged on by mighty strength, auspicious lady.

9. Looking on all created things, the goddess
Shines far and wide, facing the eye of Surya.
Awaking every living soul to motion,
She has aroused the voice of every thinker.

10. Born newly again and again though ancient,
Herself adorning with the selfsame colour,
The goddess wears away the life of mortals,
Like stakes diminished by a skilful gambler.

11. The ends of heaven disclosing, she awakens;
To distance far she banishes her sister.
Diminishing the years of life, the maiden
Flushes afar with the light of her lover.

12. Gracious and bright, spreading her rays like cattle,
As a river its flood, afar she glimmers.
Infringing not the gods' unchanging statutes,
She flushes radiant with the beams of Surya.

13. O Dawn, bring us that brilliant wealth,
O thou that bearest rich rewards,
Whereby both sons and grandsons we may well maintain.

14. Refulgent Dawn, to-day and here,
Thou that art rich in kine and steeds,
Shine forth on us abundant wealth, goddess benign.

15. Yoke, Dawn, to-day thy ruddy steeds,
O thou that bearest rich rewards:
Then on thy car to us all fortune's gifts convey.

I, 113. METRE: TRISTUBH.

1. This light has come, of all the lights the fairest:
The brilliant brightness has been born effulgent.
Urged onward for god Savitar's uprising,
Night now has yielded up her place to morning.

2. Bringing a radiant calf she comes resplendent:
To her the Black one has given up her mansions.
Akin, immortal, following each the other,
Morning and Night fare on, exchanging colours.

3. The sisters' pathway is the same, unending:
Taught by the gods alternately they tread it.
Fair-shaped, of form diverse, yet single-minded,
Morning and Night clash not, nor do they tarry.

4. Bright leader of glad sounds she shines effulgent:
Widely she has unclosed for us her portals.
Pervading all the world she shows us riches:
Dawn has awakened every living creature.

5. Men lying on the ground she wakes to action:
Some rise to seek enjoyment of great riches,
Some, seeing little, to behold the distant:
Dawn has awakened every living creature.

6. One for dominion, and for fame another;

Another is aroused for winning greatness;

Another seeks the goal of varied nurture:

Dawn has awakened every living creature.

7. Daughter of Heaven, she has appeared before us,

A maiden shining in resplendent raiment.

Thou sovereign lady of all earthly treasure,

Auspicious Dawn, shine here to-day upon us.

8. The path of those that have gone by she follows,

The first of endless dawns to come hereafter.

The living at her rising she arouses;

The dead she never wakens from their slumber.

9. O Dawn, since thou hast made them kindle Agni,

Since thou hast shone forth with the light of Surya,

Since thou the sacrificer hast awakened:

Thou hast performed among the gods good service.

10. How distant is the time when she comes midway

Between the past and those to shine in future?

The earlier dawns right willingly she follows.

Expected, she fulfils the later's wishes.

11. Gone are those mortals who in former ages

Beheld the flushing of the early morning;

We living men now look upon her shining:
Those will be born who shall hereafter see her.

12. Dispelling foes, observer of world order,
Born in due season, giver of enjoyment,
Wafting oblations, bringing wealth and fortune,
Shine brightly here to-day, O Dawn, upon us.

13. The goddess Dawn has flushed in former ages,
And here to-day the bounteous maiden flushes:
So also may she flush in days hereafter.
With powers her own she fares, immortal, ageless.

14. In the sky's framework she has gleamed with brightness;
The goddess has cast off the robe of darkness.
Rousing the world from sleep, with ruddy horses,
Dawn in her well-yoked chariot is arriving.

15. She brings upon it many bounteous blessings;
Brightly she shines and spreads her brilliant lustre.
Last of innumerable morns departed,
First of bright morns to come, has Dawn arisen.

16. Arise! The vital breath again has reached us:
Darkness has gone away and light is coming.
She leaves a pathway for the sun to travel:
We have arrived where men prolong existence.

17. The singer lauding the refulgent mornings,
Like charioteer with reins, sends forth his message:
To-day this grant thy praiser, bounteous goddess:
Life rich in offspring shine thou down upon us.

18. The dawns that shine forth for the pious mortal,
Bestowing kine and steeds and many heroes:
May these be gained by zealous Soma-pressers,
When joyous songs break forth like gusty breezes.

19. Mother of gods and Aditi's effulgence,
Banner of sacrifice, shine forth exalted.
Shine forth and look upon our prayer with favour:
Bounteous, cause fruitfulness among the people.

20. What brilliant wealth the dawns convey, auspicious,
To bless the zealous offerer of worship,
All that may Varuna and Mitra grant us,
And Aditi and Sindhu, Earth and Heaven.

RATRI

The following is the only hymn of the Rigveda in which, under the name of Ratri, the goddess of night is invoked. Like her sister, Usas, she is a daughter of Heaven. She is conceived not as the dark, but as the bright, starlit night, shining with her eyes. Decked with all splendour, she drives away the darkness. At her approach, men, beasts and birds go to rest. Protecting her worshippers from the wolf and the thief, she guides them to safety. Under the name of nakta combined with ufas, Night appears as a dual divinity with Dawn in some twenty scattered stanzas of the Rigveda.

X, 127. METRE: GAYATRI.

1. When night comes on, the goddess shines
In many places with her eyes:
All glorious she has decked herself.

2. Immortal goddess far and wide,
She fills the valleys and the heights:
Darkness she drives away with light.

3. The goddess now, as she comes on,
Is turning out her sister, Dawn:
Far off the darkness hastes away.

4. So, goddess, come to-day to us:
At thy approach we seek our homes,
As birds their nests upon the tree.

5. The villagers have gone to rest
And footed beasts and winged birds;
The hungry hawk himself is still.

6. Ward off from us she-wolf and wolf,
Ward off the robber, goddess Night:
So take us safe across the gloom.

7. The darkness, thickly painting black,
Has, palpable, come nigh to me:
Like debts, O Dawn, clear it away.

8. I have brought up a hymn, like kine,
For thee, as one who wins a fight:
This, Heaven's daughter, Night, accept.

THE AVINS

Next to Indra, Agni and Soma, the twin deities, called Asvins, "Horsemen," are the most prominent gods in the Rigveda, being invoked in more than 50 entire hymns and in parts of several others. The time of their appearance is between dawn and sunrise, when darkness still abides among the ruddy cows (i.e. the rays of dawn). Usas awakens them; she is followed by them on their car. They dispel darkness and drive away evil spirits. Their car, which was fashioned by the three divine artificers, the Rbhus, and is sunlike and golden, is threefold and has three wheels. It is drawn by horses, or by birds, or by winged steeds. Its revolving course traverses heaven and earth in one day. The Asvins are the children of Heaven, but are once called the sons of Vivasvant (the sun) and Saranyu (probably the dawn). Pusan is once said to be their son, and Dawn is probably meant by their sister. They are often associated with the daughter of the sun, Surya, who rides with them on their car and is their spouse.

The Asvins are twins and inseparable. They are young and yet ancient, handsome, lords of lustre, of golden brightness, adorned with lotus garlands, and they follow a golden path. They are more closely associated than any of the other gods with mead (madhu), which they desire and drink. But they are also fond of Soma, which they drink with Usas and Surya. They possess profound wisdom and occult power, but their two most frequent epithets are "wondrous" and "true." Typically rescuers from distress, they are divine physicians, who cure diseases with their remedies, healing the sick and maimed, and restoring youth and sight. Many legends are told of those whom they befriended, especially that of Bhujyu, whom they saved in a ship from the ocean. The meaning of their name is "the two horsemen," not, however, as riders, but as charioteers. They evidently belong to the group of the deities of light, but the actual phenomenon which they represent is doubtful. The two most probable theories are that they originally represented either the morning twilight, as half light and half dark, or the morning and evening star. They probably go back to the Indo-European period, being akin to the two famous horsemen of Greek mythology, the sons of Zeus, brothers of Helena; and to the two Lettic god's sons, who come riding on their steeds to woo the daughter of the sun.

VIII, 71. METRE: TRISTUBH.

1. Night hastens far away from Dawn, her sister;

The Black one yields the ruddy god a pathway.

We call on you two rich in kine and horses:

By day and night ward off from us the arrow.

2. Come to the pious mortal bringing bounty,
O Asvins, hither with your chariot speeding.
Do ye ward off from us disease and weakness.
By day and night, lovers of sweetness, guard us.

3. May your propitious coursers whirl your chariot
Toward us at the dawn now flushing on us.
Bring it, by traces drawn and fraught with riches,
Hither with horses yoked by Order, Asvins.

4. That car, three-seated, lords of men, that bears you
With riches laden well, drives forth at daybreak:
On it, O Nasatyas, to us come onward,
That, with all nurture fraught, it may approach us.

5. Once from old age ye two released Chyavana;
With a swift courser ye presented Pedu;

Ye rescued Atri from distress and darkness;
The fettered Jahusha ye placed in freedom.

6. To you this thought, this song is offered, Asvins,
This hymn of praise enjoy, ye mighty heroes.
From us these prayers have gone, to you directed.
Ye gods protect us evermore with blessings.

INDRA

Indra, being the favourite national god of the Vedic people, is invoked in about one-fourth of the hymns of the Rigveda in far more than are addressed to any other deity. He is more anthropomorphic and more invested with mythological imagery than any other Vedic god. He is primarily a deity of the thunderstorm, who vanquishes the demons of drought or darkness, setting free the waters or winning the light. His physical parts, such as his body and his head, are often mentioned. His form, as well as his hair and his beard, is tawny. His two arms are especially often referred to as wielding the thunderbolt (vafra), which is his exclusive weapon. This missile, fashioned for him by the artificer god, Tvastar, is made of iron, but sometimes of stone, is sharp and many-pointed, and golden or tawny in colour. Sometimes he is armed with bow and arrows, and he also carries a hook. His golden car is drawn by two tawny steeds. Indra is, more than any other god, addicted to Soma, which stimulates him to carry out his warlike deeds, especially the slaughter of the demon Vrtra. One entire hymn consists of a monologue in which Indra, intoxicated with Soma, boasts of his greatness and his might. The inference from some hymns is that his father is Dyaus (Heaven), but from others that he is Tvastar. Agni and Pusan are his brothers. His wife, often mentioned, is Indrani. He is associated with various other deities. The Maruts, or storm gods, are his chief allies in conflicts. Agni is the god most often conjoined with him as a dual divinity. He is often also coupled with Varuna and Vayu, less often with Soma, Brhaspati, Pusan and Visnu. Indra is described as vast in size. His greatness and power are constantly dwelt on and emphasized by various epithets applied to him exclusively. The essential myth that forms the basis of his nature is described with great frequency and much variation. Exhilarated by Soma and generally accompanied by the Maruts, Indra attacks the chief demon of drought, usually called Vrtra, but also often the serpent. Heaven and earth tremble when the mighty combat takes place. With his bolt he shatters Vrtra, who encompasses the waters. The result of the conflict, which is regarded as being constantly renewed, is that Indra pierces the mountain and sets free the waters pent up like imprisoned cows. The physical elements in the conflict are nearly always the bolt, mountains, waters or rivers, while lightning, thunder, cloud, rain are seldom directly named. The waters are often terrestrial, but also aerial and celestial. The clouds are the mountains on which the demons lie or dwell, or from which he casts them down, or which he cleaves to release the waters. Or the cloud is a rock which encompasses the cows (as the waters are sometimes called), and from which he sets them free. Clouds, as holding the waters, figure as cows also; they appear, moreover, under the names of udder, spring, cask, or pail. The clouds further figure as the fortresses of the aerial demons, being described as moving, autumnal, made of iron or stone, and as ninety, ninety-nine, or a hundred in number. Indra, who shatters them, is therefore called the "fort-destroyer." But his chief and specific epithet is "Vrtra-slayer," as expressing his main activity. In his fight with the demon the Maruts are his regular allies, though Agni, Soma, and Visnu also often assist him. Indra also fights with various minor demons; sometimes he destroys demons in general

(Raksases or Asuras). With the release of the waters is connected the winning of light, sun and dawn. Thus Indra is invoked to slay Vrtra and to win the light. When he had slain Vrtra and released the waters for man, he placed the sun visibly in the heavens. The sun shone forth when Indra blew the serpent from the air. In this connexion there is often no mention of the Vrtra fight. Indra is then simply said to find the light; he gained the sun or found it in the darkness, making a path for it. He produces the dawn as well as the sun; he opens the darkness with the dawn and the sun. The cows mentioned along with the sun and dawn, or with the sun alone, as found or won by Indra, are here probably the morning beams, which are elsewhere compared with cattle coming out of their dark stalls. Thus when the dawns went to meet Indra, he became the lord of the cows; when he overcame Vrtra, he made visible the cows of the nights. There seems to be a confusion between the restoration of the sun after the darkness of the thunderstorm and the recovery of the sun from the darkness of night at dawn. The latter feature is probably an extension of the former. With the Vrtra fight and the winning of the cows and of the sun, is also connected the gaining of Soma. Thus when Indra drove the serpent from the air, there shone forth fires, the sun, and the Soma; he won Soma at the same time as the cows.

Great cosmic actions are often ascribed to Indra: he settled the quaking mountains and plains; he stretches out heaven and earth like a hide; he holds asunder heaven and earth; he turned the non-existent into the existent in a moment. As the destroyer of demons in combat, Indra is constantly invoked by warriors. As the great god of battle he is more frequently called upon than any other deity to help the Aryans in their conflicts with earthly enemies. He protects the Aryan colour and subjects the black skin. He dispersed 50,000 of the black race. He subjected the Dasyus to the Aryan, on whom he bestowed land. More generally, Indra is the protector, helper and friend of his worshippers. He grants them wealth, regarded as the result of victories. His liberality is so characteristic that the epithet "Bountiful" (maghavan) is almost exclusively restricted to him. Several minor myths are connected with Indra. One of them is that of the winning of Soma: it is to him that the eagle brings the draught of immortality from the highest heaven. Another is the capture by Indra, with the help of Sarama, of the cows confined in a cave by demons called Panis. Moreover, various stories containing mythological elements, but probably having a historical foundation, are told about Indra's fighting in aid of individual men, such as king Sudas, against terrestrial foes. Indra forms a striking contrast to Varuna, the other divine universal monarch of the Rigveda. His attributes are mainly those of physical superiority, and rule over the physical world. He is violent in action, an irresistible warrior, a lavisher of spoils on mankind, but also sensual and immoral in various ways, such as excess in eating and drinking, and cruelty in killing his father, Tvastar. Varuna, on the other hand, wields passive and peaceful sway, applies the laws of nature with uniformity, upholds moral order, and in his character displays lofty ethical features. Indra is pre-Vedic, for his name occurs in the Avesta as that of demon; and the term Vrtra-slayer, as a designation of the god of Victory, occurs there, though unconnected with Indra. It is therefore probable that there was already in the Indo-Iranian period a god resembling the Vrtra-slaying Indra of the Rigveda.

I, 32. METRE: TRISTUBH.

1. I will proclaim the manly deeds of Indra,
The first that he performed, the lightning-wielder.
He slew the serpent, then discharged the waters,
And cleft the caverns of the lofty mountains.

2. He slew the serpent lying on the mountain:
For him the whizzing bolt has Tvastar fashioned.
Like lowing cows, with rapid current flowing,
The waters to the ocean down have glided.

3. Impetuous like a bull he chose the Soma,
And drank in threefold vessels of its juices.
The bounteous god grasped lightning for his missile;
He struck down dead that first-born of the serpents.

4. When thou hadst slain the first-born of the serpents,
And thwarted all the wiles of crafty schemers,
Anon disclosing sun, and dawn, and heaven,
Thou truly foundest not a foe, O Indra.

5. Indra slew Vrtra and one worse than Vrtra,
Vyamsa, with lightning, his resistless weapon:
Like trunks of trees, with axes hewn in pieces,
The serpent clinging to the earth lay prostrate.

6. He like a drunken coward challenged Indra,
The headlong, many-crushing, mighty hero.
He parried not the onset of the weapons;
The foe of Indra, falling, crushed the channels.

7. Footless and handless he with Indra battled,
Who smote him then upon his back with lightning.
But, impotent, he strove to match the hero:
He lay with scattered limbs in many places.

8. As thus he lay, like broken reed, the waters,
Now courage taking, surge across his body.
He lies beneath the very feet of rivers
Which Vrtra with his might had close encompassed.

9. The strength began to fail of Vrtra's mother,
For Indra had cast down his bolt upon her.
Above the mother was, the son was under;
And like a cow beside her calf lies Danu.

10. The waters deep have hidden Vrtra's body,
Plunged in the midst of never-ceasing torrents
That stand not still, but ever hasten onward:
Indra's fierce foe sank down to lasting darkness.

11. Enclosed by demons, guarded by a serpent,
The waters stood like oows by Pani captured.

The waters' orifice that was obstructed,
When Vrtra he had smitten, Indra opened.
12. A horse's tail thou didst become, O Indra,
When, on his spear impaled, as god unaided,
The cows, O hero, thou didst win and Soma,
And free the seven streams to flow in torrents.

13. Him lightning then availed not nor thunder,
Nor mist, nor hailstorm which around he scattered:
When Indra and the serpent fought in battle,
The bounteous god gained victory for ever.

14. Whom saw'st thou as avenger of the serpent,
As terror seized thy heart when thou hadst slain him,
And thou didst cross the nine and ninety rivers
And air's broad spaces, like a hawk affrighted?

15. Indra is king of all that's fixed and moving,
Of tame and horned beasts, the thunder-wielder.
He truly rules, as king of busy mortals;
Them he encompasses as spokes the felly.

PARJANYA

Parjanya is a subordinate deity in the Rigveda, being invoked in three hymns only. He is a rain-god. The name often means "rain-cloud," but generally represents its personification. It is often alluded to as an udder, a pail, or a water-skin. Parjanya is frequently spoken of as a bull that quickens the plants and the earth. The shedding of rain is his most prominent characteristic: he flies around with a watery car and loosens the water-skin, shedding rain-water as our divine father; he is then associated with thunder and lightning. He is in a special degree a nourisher of vegetation, and also a producer of animal fertility. He is several times called a father. He is once said to be the son of heaven, and his wife is by implication the earth.

V, 83. METRE: l_.5-8, 10 TRISTUBH;

2-4 JAGATI; 9 ANUTUBH.

1. Invoke the mighty god with songs of welcome;

Parjanya praise: with homage seek to win him.

He, roaring like a bull, with streams that quicken,

A seed to germinate in plants deposits.

2. The trees he shatters and he smites the demon host:

The whole world trembles at his mighty weapon's stroke,

The guiltless man himself flees from the potent god,

When miscreants Parjanya with his thunder strikes.

3. Like charioteer his horses lashing with a whip,

The god makes manifest his messengers of rain. .

From far away the roaring of the lion sounds,

What time Parjanya veils the firmament with rain.

4. The winds blow forth; to earth the quivering lightning fall,
The plants shoot up; with moisture streams the realm of light.
For all the world abundant nourishment is born,
When by Parjanya Earth is fertilized with seed.

5. O thou at whose behest the earth bows downward,
O thou at whose behest hoofed creatures quiver,
At whose behest by plants all shapes are taken:
As such, Parjanya, grant to us strong shelter.

6. The rain of heaven bestow, O Maruts, on us,
Of your strong steed pour forth the streams abundant.
With this thy thundering roar do thou come hither,
And shed the waters as our heavenly father.

7. With roar and thunder now the germ deposit,
Fly round us with thy water-bearing chariot.
Turn well thy water-skin unloosened downward,
Make, with the waters, heights and hollows level.

8. Draw the great bucket up and pour it downward,
And let the liberated streams flow forward.
On all sides drench both heaven and earth with fatness;
Let there be for the cows fair pools for drinking.

9. When, O Parjanya, roaring loud,
Thou slay'st with thunder wicked men,
This universe rejoices then,
And everything that is on earth.

10. Thou hast shed rain; pray now withhold it wholly;
Thou hast made passable all desert places.
To serve as food thou hast made plants to flourish:
And hast received the gratitude of creatures.

RUDRA

Rudra is invoked alone in only three entire hymns. His hand, his arms, and his limbs are mentioned, and he is described as having beautiful lips and braided hair. He is brown in colour and shines like the radiant sun, being arrayed in golden ornaments and wearing a glorious necklace. He drives in a car; he holds the thunderbolt in his arm, and discharges his lightning shaft from the sky; but he is usually armed with a bow and arrows. Rudra is often associated with the Maruts, whose father he is. He is fierce and destructive like a terrible beast, being called a bull and the ruddy boar of heaven. He is unsurpassed in might, young and unaging, a lord and father of the world. By his rule and universal dominion he is aware of the doings of men and gods. He is bountiful, easily invoked and auspicious. But he is usually malevolent; for the hymns addressed to him chiefly express fear of his terrible shafts and deprecation of his wrath. He is implored not to slay or injure, in his anger, his worshippers and their belongings, but to avert his great malignity and his cow-slaying, manslaying bolt from them. But he is not purely maleficent like a demon. He not only preserves from calamity, but bestows blessings. His healing powers are often mentioned. He has a thousand remedies and is the greatest of physicians. The phenomenon underlying Rudra's nature is not quite clear; but it was probably the storm, not pure and simple, but in its baleful aspect as manifested in the destructive agency of lightning. His healing and beneficent powers would then have been founded partly on the fertilizing and purifying action of the thunderstorm, and partly on the negative action of sparing those whom he might slay. Thus the deprecations of his wrath led to the application to him of the euphemistic epithet, Siva, "Auspicious," the regular name of Rudra's historical successor in post-Vedic mythology.

II, 33. METRE: TRISTUBH

1. Let thy goodwill, O father of the Maruts,

Light on us: part us not from Surya's vision.

In mercy may the hero spare our horses:

May we, O Rudra, have abundant offspring.

2. By thy most wholesome remedies, O Rudra,

Thy gifts, I would attain a hundred autumns.

Drive far away from us distress and hatred,

Drive far away, wide-scattered, all diseases.

3. Of what is born thou art the chief in glory,
Armed with the thunder, mightiest of the mighty.
Transport us to the farther shore of trouble
In safety; frustrate all attacks of mischief.

4. May we not anger thee with homage, Rudra,
Nor with ill-praises, nor joint invocation.
Raise up, O Bull, with remedies our heroes:
I hear of thee as best of all physicians.

5. With invocations and oblations summoned
Rudra I would appease with my laudations:
May he, soft-hearted, easily appealed to,
Brown-hued, fair-lipped, not to his wrath subject us.

6. The bull, escorted by the Maruts, gladdens
Me who invokes, with his most forceful vigour.
I, sound, would reach, as in the heat, a shelter:
Rudra's good will I would desire to capture.

7. Where is that gracious hand of thine, O Rudra,
That is so full of remedies and coolness?
As the remover of all god-sent damage,
Do thou, O Bull, now show compassion towards me.

8. Forth for the brown and whitish bull I utter
A mighty panegyric of the mighty.
I will adore the radiant god with homage.
We praise the terrifying name of Rudra.

9. He, mighty, brown-hued, multiform, has decked out
His stalwart limbs with jewels bright and golden,
From Rudra, this great universe's ruler,
Let not be severed his divine dominion.

10. Worthy, thou carriest thy bow and arrows,
Worthy, thine honoured and all-hued necklace
Worthy, thou wieldest all this mighty power.
Naught that exists is mightier than thou art.

11. Praise him the famed, who sits upon the car-seat
The young, the fierce, like a dread beast, a slayer.
When praised, be gracious, Rudra, to the singer:
Let thy darts pass us and lay low another.

12. I bow down like a son before his father,
Who with good will comes nigh to him, O Rudra.
I praise the true lord, of much wealth the giver:
To us thou grantest remedies when lauded.

13. Those remedies of yours, the pure, O Maruts,
That are most wholesome, mighty ones, and potent,
That Manu chose in ancient days, our Father:
Those I desire, and Rudra's balm and blessing.

14. May Rudra's missile turn aside and pass us,
May the fierce Rudra's great ill-will go by us.
Relax thy rigid bow to save our patrons;
Spare, O thou god of bounty, child and grandchild.

15. So brown-hued, mighty Rudra, widely famous,
Here to our invocations be attentive,
As not, O god, to rise in wrath and slay us.
May we speak loud with heroes in the synod.

MARUTS

The Maruts, or Storm-gods, are prominent deities in the Rigveda, being invoked in 33 hymns alone, and in 9 others in association with other gods (Indra, Agni, Pusan). They form a group, being mentioned in the plural only. Their number is stated as thrice seven or thrice sixty. They are the sons of Rudra and Prsni (who probably represents the mottled storm-cloud). But they are also said to have been generated by Vayu, god of wind, or to be the sons of heaven, or even to be self-born. They are brothers of equal age, having the same birthplace and abode. The goddess Rodasi is always connected with them as riding on their car. She seems to have been regarded as their bride. The brilliance of the Maruts is characteristic, and they are very frequently associated with lightning. They have spears of lightning and wear golden helmets. They are armed with golden axes, but sometimes with bows and arrows, like their father Rudra. They wear golden mantles, and golden ornaments, garlands, armlets and anklets. Their cars gleam with lightning, being drawn by steeds (generally feminine) that are ruddy, tawny, or spotted. The noise made by the Maruts, often mentioned, is thunder and the roaring of the winds. They cause the mountains to quake and the two worlds to tremble; they shatter trees and, like wild elephants, devour the forests. They are often called singers: they sing a song; they are the singers of heaven; for Indra, when he slew the dragon, they sang a song and pressed Soma. Their song, though primarily representing the sound of the winds, is also conceived as a hymn of praise. Thus they come to be compared with priests and are even addressed as such.

One of the main activities of the Maruts is to shed rain: they cover the eye of the sun with rain; they create darkness with the cloud when they shed rain; they cause the celestial pail and the streams of the mountains to pour. The waters shed by them are often clearly connected with the thunderstorm. Their rain is often figuratively called milk, ghee, or honey. They avert heat, but also dispel darkness, produce light, and prepare a path for the sun. More generally the Maruts are described as young and unaging, dustless, mighty, fierce, terrible like lions, but also playful like children or calves.

Owing to their connexion with the thunderstorm, the Maruts are constantly associated with Indra as his friends and allies, who increase his strength and his prowess with their songs, prayers, and hymns, and generally assist him in his fight with Vrtra. Indra, in fact, accomplishes all his celestial feats in their company. But sometimes the Maruts accomplish these same feats alone.

When they are not associated with Indra, the Maruts occasionally exhibit the maleficent traits of their father Rudra. Hence they are implored to ward off their lightning from their worshippers and not to let their ill-will reach them, and are besought to avert their arrow and the stone which they hurl, their lightning, and their cow- and man-slaying bolt. But, like their father Rudra, they are also supplicated to bring healing remedies. These remedies appear to be the waters, for the Maruts bestow medicine by raining. The evidence of the Rigveda shows that the Maruts are storm-gods. Etymologically the word may mean either the "Shiners" or the "Crushers."

VIII, 7. METRE: GAYATRI.

1. When, Maruts, now for you the sage
Pours out the threefold Soma draught,
Ye shine forth on the mountain heights.

2. Whenever, bright ones, growing strong,
You have decided on your course,
The mountains bend and bow themselves.

3. Loud roaring with the winds, the sons
Of Prsni raise themselves aloft:
They have milked out the swelling draught.

4. The Maruts scatter mist abroad,
They make the mountain ridges quake,
When with the winds they go their way.

5. When mountains bow before your march,
And rivers, too, before your rule,
Before your mighty, roaring blast:

6. On you we call by night for aid
On you we call aloud by day,
On you while sacrifice proceeds.

7. They rise, of ruddy hue and bright,
Upon their courses with a roar,
Across the ridges of the sky.

8. With power they shoot a ray of light
So that the sun may run his course;
They with their beams spread far and wide.

9. Accept, O Maruts, this my song,
Rbhuksans, this my hymn of praise,
Accept ye now this call of mine.

10. The dappled cows have milked three lakes,
Mead for the wielder of the bolt,
Out of the spring, the water-cask.

11. O Maruts, pray come here to us,
Whenever, seeking your good will,
We call you hither from the sky.

12. For, Rudras and Rbhuksans, ye,
O bounteous ones, are in our house
And wise when ye enjoy the draught.

13. From heaven, Maruts, bring to us
Abundant wealth distilling joy,
With plenteous food all-nourishing.

14. When you, as if from mountain tops,
Have, bright ones, willed to take your way,
You in the drops distilled rejoice.

15. The mortal with his prayers should ask
The favour and goodwill of that
Great host of theirs invincible.

VATA

The god of Wind is invoked by the two names of Vayu and Vata, both derived from the root va, "to blow." The former is addressed in one whole hymn and parts of others, the latter in two short hymns. Both names are sometimes used in the same verse, but Vayu is more often the god, Vata the element. In keeping with the latter distinction, Vayu is often associated with the anthropomorphic Indra as a dual divinity, while Vata is similarly coupled with Parjanya, whose connexion with the thunderstorm is more vivid and realistic than that of Indra. Different sets of epithets are applied to these two wind-gods. Vayu has a shining car drawn by a team or by a pair of ruddy steeds. He is fond of Soma, and is its protector. He grants fame, offspring and wealth; he disperses foes and protects the weak. Vata is the breath of the gods; like Rudra he wafts healing and prolongs life, for he has the treasure of immortality in his house. He is chiefly mentioned in connexion with the thunderstorm, and his noise is often referred to. He produces ruddy lights and makes the dawns to shine. His swiftness often supplies a comparison for the speed of the gods or of mythical steeds.

X, 168. METRE: TRISTUBH.

1. Of Vata's car I now will praise the greatness:

Rending it speeds along; its noise is thunder.

Touching the sky it flies, creating lightnings;

Scattering dust it traverses earth's ridges.

2. The hosts of Vata onward speed together:

They haste to him as women to a concourse.

The god with them upon the same car mounted,

The king of all this universe speeds onward.

3. In air, along his pathways speeding onward,

Never on any day he tarries resting.

The first-born order-loving friend of waters:

Where was he born, and whence has he arisen?

4. Of gods the breath, and of the world the offspring,

This god according to his liking wanders.

His sound is heard, his form is never looked on:

That Vata let us worship with oblation.

APAS: WATERS

The waters, which are invoked in four entire hymns, as well as in a few detached stanzas, are personified only to the extent of being thought of as mothers, young wives and goddesses, bestowing boons and coming to the sacrifice. They follow the path of the gods. They flow in a channel dug out with his bolt by Indra, whose ordinances they never infringe. The sea is their goal. But they are also celestial; for their abode is with the gods, in the seat of Mitra-Varuna, beside the sun. King Varuna moves in their midst, looking down on the truth and falsehood of men. As mothers they produce not only Agni, but all that is fixed or moves. They purify and carry away defilement. They also cleanse from moral guilt from the sins of violence, cursing and lying. They further bestow remedies, health, strength, long life, wealth and im- mortality. Their favour is often invoked, and they are invited to receive the Soma libation, seated on the sacrificial grass. The waters are often associated with honey: their milk mixed with honey is produced in the sky, gladdens the gods, and became the drink of Indra, giving him heroic strength. Here the celestial waters seem to be identified with the heavenly Soma. Elsewhere the waters used in preparing the terrestrial Soma seem to be meant. Thus they appear, bearing ghee and honey, in accord with the priests that bring well-pressed Soma for Indra. Soma delights in them as a young man in lovely maidens. He approaches them as a lover; before him, the youth, they, the maidens, bow down. The deification of the waters is pre-Vedic, for they are invoked in the Avesta also. VII, 49. METRE: TRISTUBH.

1. With ocean for their chief they flow unresting;

From the aerial flood they hasten cleansing;

For whom the mighty Indra's bolt cut channels,

Here may those waters, goddesses, preserve me.

2. Waters that come from heaven or run in channels

Dug out, or flow spontaneously by nature,

That, clear and pure, have as their goal the ocean;

Here may those waters, goddesses, preserve me.

3. In midst of whom king Varuna is moving,
And looking down surveys men's truth and falsehood:
Who, clear and purifying, drip with sweetness:
Here may those waters, goddesses, preserve me.

4. In whom king Varuna, in whom, too, Soma,
In whom the All-gods drink exalted vigour;
Into whom Agni, friend of all, has entered:
Here may those waters, goddesses, preserve me.

APAM NAPAT

Apam Napat, the Son of Waters, is invoked in one entire hymn and is often incidentally mentioned elsewhere. He is youthful and brilliant, shining without fuel in the waters that surround and nourish him. Clothed with lightning he is of golden aspect, shining with undimmed splendour in the highest place. He is borne by steeds swift as thought. In the last stanza of the following hymn he is invoked as Agni, who, moreover, is called Apam Napat in an Agni hymn; the epithet, "swiftly-speeding," is further applied to these two deities exclusively, though they are otherwise sometimes distinguished. Apam Napat thus appears to represent the lightning form of Agni hidden in the cloud. For Agni is not only directly called Apam Napat, but also described as the "embryo of the waters"; the third form of Agni is, moreover, said to be kindled in the waters. This god is an inheritance from pre-Indian mythology, for in the Avesta Apam Napat is a spirit of the waters who lives in their depths, surrounded by females and often invoked with them, who drives with swift steeds, and is associated with brilliance in the depth of the ocean.

II, 35. METRE: TRISTUBH.

1. Desiring gain this eloquence I utter:
May the streams' son accept my songs with gladness.
Will he, the Son of Waters, of swift impulse,
Perchance reward them well? He will enjoy them.

2. Now from our hearts we would this hymn well-fashioned
Address to him: perchance he will regard it.
The noble Son of Waters, by the greatness
Of rule divine, all creatures has created.

3. Some flow together, some approach the ocean;
The rivers thus fill up the common cistern.
And him the pure, the shining Son of Waters,
The waters pure on all sides have surrounded.

4. The waters, youthful maidens, never smiling,
Making him bright, encompass him the youthful.
He with clear flames, free-handedly upon us,
Unfed with wood, shines decked with ghee in waters.

5. Three dames divine to him the god, the dauntless,
Wish eagerly to offer food for nurture.
He seems to seek their breasts within the waters:
He drinks the milk of them that first are mothers.

6. The birthplace of this steed is earth and heaven.
Our patrons do thou guard from harm and malice.
Him not to be forgotten, far off dwelling
In cloud-built forts, foes shall not reach nor falsehoods.

7. He in whose house is a productive milch-cow
Increasing vital force, fares on good nurture.
The Waters' Son, expanding in the waters,
Shines forth upon the pious, granting riches.

8. Who in the waters, with celestial brightness,
Shines widely forth, eternal, law-abiding,
Of him as branches every plant and creature
Do propagate themselves with all their offspring.

PRTHIVI: EARTH

The following hymn is the only one in the Rigveda to Prthivi, Earth, though she is often celebrated with Dyaus, Heaven, conjointly (.e.g. p. 67), as a dual divinity. There is also a long and beautiful hymn addressed to Prthivi in the Atharvaveda. The personification is but slight, as the attributes of the goddess are chiefly those of the physical earth. In a funeral hymn she is spoken of as "Kindly mother Earth," and when mentioned with Dyaus she frequently receives the epithet of "Mother." The name means "The broad one," being derived, as indicated in the Rigveda itself, from the root prath, "To extend."

V, 84. METRE: ANUSTUBH.

1. Thou bearest truly, Prithvi,
The burden of the mountains' weight;
With might, O thouof many streams,
Thou quickenest, potent one, the soil,

2. With flowers of speech our songs of praise
Resound to thee, far-spreading one,
Who sendest forth the swelling cloud,
O bright one, like propelling speed;

3. Who, steadfast, boldest with thy might,
The forest-trees upon the ground,
When, from the lightning of thy cloud,
The rain-floods of the sky pour down.

DYAVA-PRTHIVI

Heaven and Earth are the most frequently named pair in the Rigveda. They are so closely associated that, while they are invoked as a couple in six hymns, Dyaus, Heaven, is never addressed alone in any hymn, and Prthivi, Earth, in only one of three stanzas. The two deities are quite co-ordinate, while in most of the other couples, one of the two greatly predominates. Thus they probably represent the prototype of the class of dual divinities in the Rigveda. They are parents besides being separately addressed as "father" and "mother." They have made and sustain all creatures, being also the parents of the gods. One of them is called a prolific bull, the other a varigated cow. They never grow old. Great and far-extended they are broad and vast abodes. They grant food and wealth, bestowing fame and dominion. They are wise and promote righteousness. As parents they guard creatures and protect from disgrace and misfortune. They are sufficiently personified to be called leaders of the sacrifice and to be thought of as seating themselves around the offering; but they never attained to a living personification or importance in worship.

I, 185. METRE: TRISTUBH.

1. Which of the two is earlier, which the later?

How were they born, ye sages, who discerns it?

They by themselves support all things existing.

As with a wheel the day and night roll onward.

2. The two support, though moving not and footless,

Abundant offspring having feet and moving.

O Heaven and Earth, from dreadful darkness save us,

Like your own son held in his parents' bosom.

3. I crave of Aditi the gift, the matchless,
Beneficent, illustrious, and honoured:
O ye two worlds, procure that for the singer.
O Heaven and Earth, from dreadful darkness save us.

4. May we be near to both the worlds who suffer
No care, parents of gods, who aid with favour.
Both are divine, with days and nights alternate.
O Heaven and Earth from dreadful darkness save us.

5. Maidens uniting, with adjoining limits,
Twin sisters, resting in their parents' bosom,
They kiss, combined, the universe's centre.
O Heaven and Earth, from dreadful darkness save us.

6. Devoutly I the two seats wide and lofty,
The parents of the gods, invoke with fervour,
Who, fair of aspect, grant us life immortal.
Heaven and Earth, from dreadful darkness save us.

7. Them wide and broad and great, whose bounds are distant,
Who, beautiful and fain to help, grant blessings:
I at this sacrifice invoke with homage.
O Heaven and Earth, from dreadful darkness save us.

8. If ever we have any sin committed
Against the gods, or friend, or house's chieftain,
Of that may this our hymn be expiation.
O Heaven and Earth, from dreadful darkness save us.

9. May both, as objects of men's praises, bless me;
May both attend me with their help and favour,
Give much to men more liberal than the godless.
We would be strong, ye gods, enjoying nurture.

10. This truth have I now uttered first with wisdom
To Heaven and Earth that every one may hear it.
Protect me from disgrace and peril: guard me
As Father and as Mother with your succour.

11. May this my prayer come true, O Earth and Heaven,
With which I here address you, Father, Mother.
Be nearest of the gods to us with favours:
May we find food and home with flowing water.

AGNI

Agni and Soma are the two great ritual deities of the Rigveda. Judged by the number of hymns addressed to him, Agni is second in importance to Indra only, being invoked in at least 200. His anthropomorphism is only rudimentary, being connected chiefly with the sacrificial aspect of fire. He is butter-backed, flame-haired, has a tawny beard, sharp jaws, and golden teeth. His tongue, with which the gods eat the oblation, is often mentioned. With a burning head he faces in all directions. Agni is compared with various animals: he resembles a bellowing bull, and sharpens his horns; when born he is often called a calf; when kindled he is like a horse that brings the gods, and is yoked to convey the sacrifice to them. He is also a divine bird; he is the eagle of the sky; as dwelling in the waters he is like a goose; he is winged and takes possession of the wood, as a bird perches on a tree. Wood or ghee is his food, melted butter his drink, and he is nourished three times a day. He is the mouth by which the gods eat the sacrifice; and his flames are spoons with which he besprinkles the gods; he is also asked to consume the offerings himself. Agni's brightness is much dwelt on: he shines like the sun; his lustre is like the rays of the dawn and the sun, and resembles the lightnings of the rain-cloud. He shines even at night, and dispels the darkness with his beams. On the other hand, his path is black when he invades the forests and shaves the earth as a barbei a beard. His flames are like roaring waves, and his sound is like the thunder of heaven. His red smoke rises up to the firmament; like the erector of a post he supports the sky with his smoke. "Smoke-bannered" is his frequent and exclusive epithet. He has a shining, golden, lightning car, drawn by two or more ruddy or tawny steeds. He is the charioteer of sacrifice, and with his steeds he brings the gods on his car. Agni is the child of Heaven, and is often called the son of Heaven and Earth. He is also the offspring of the waters. Indra is called Agni's twin brother, and is more closely associated with him than any other god. The mythology of Agni, apart from his sacrificial activity, is mostly concerned with his various births, forms and abodes. Mention is often made of his daily production from the two kindling sticks, which are his parents. From the dry wood Agni is born: as soon as born the child devours his parents. The ten fingers of the kindler are called the ten maidens. Owing to the force needed to kindle him, he is spoken of as the "Son of Strength." Being produced every morning, he is young; at the same time no sacrificer is older than he: for he conducted the first sacrifice. Secondly, Agni's origin in the aerial waters is often referred to: he is an embryo of the waters; he is kindled in the waters; he is a bull that has grown in the lap of the waters. As "Son of Waters" he has become a separate deity. He is also sometimes conceived as latent in terrestrial waters. This notion of Agni in the waters is a prominent one in the Rigveda. Thirdly, a celestial origin of Agni is often mentioned: he is born in the highest heaven, and was brought down from heaven by Matarisvan, the Indian Prometheus; and the acquisition of fire by man is regarded as a gift of the gods as well as a production of Matarisvan. The Sun is, moreover, regarded as a form of Agni. Thus Agni is the light of heaven in the bright sky; he was born on the other side of the air, and sees all things; he is born as the sun rising in the morning. Hence Agni comes to have a triple character: his births are three, or three-fold; the gods made him threefold; he is threefold light; he has three heads, three bodies, three stations. The threefold nature of Agni is clearly recognised in the Rigveda, and represents the earliest Indian trinity. The universe being also regarded as consisting of the two divisions of heaven and earth, Agni is said to have two origins, and indeed is the only god described as "having two births." As kindled in numerous dwellings, Agni is said to have many births. He is more closely associated with human life than any other deity, being the only god called ' Lord of the house" and constantly spoken of as a guest in human dwellings. He is an immortal who has taken up his abode among mortals. Thus he comes to be termed the nearest kinsman of man. He is oftenest described as a father, sometimes also as a brother, or even as a son of his worshippers. He both takes the offerings of men to the gods and brings the gods to the sacrifice. He is thus characteristically a messenger appointed by gods and by men to be an "oblation-bearer." As the centre of the sacrifice Agni comes to be celebrated as the divine counterpart of the earthly priesthood. Hence he is often called "priest," "domestic priest," and, more often than by any other name, "invoking priest" (/ wtar), less often "officiating priest" and "praying priest." His priesthood is the most salient feature of his character: he is, in fact, the great priest as Indra is the great warrior. Agni's wisdom is often dwelt upon: as knowing all the details of sacrifice, he is wise and omniscient, being exclusively called "knower of all created beings." He is a great benefactor of his worshippers, bestowing on them all kinds of boons, especially domestic welfare, offspring, and general prosperity, His greatness is often celebrated, being once even said to surpass that of the other gods. His cosmic and creative powers are also frequently praised. From the ordinary sacrificial Agni, who conveys the offering, is distinguished his "corpse-devouring" form, that burns the body on the funeral pyre. Another function of Agni is to burn and dispel evil spirits and hostile magic.

The sacrificial fire was already in the Indo-Iranian period the centre of a developed ritual, being personified and worshipped as a mighty, wise and beneficent god. It seems to have been an Indo-European institution also, since the Greeks and Romans, as well as the Indians and Iranians, had the custom of offering gifts to the gods in fire. But whether it was already personified in that remote period is a matter of conjecture.

1,1. METRE: GAYATRI.

1. Agni I praise, the household priest,

God, minister of sacrifice,

Invoker, best bestowing wealth.

2. Agni is worthy to be praised,
By present as by seers of old:
May he to us conduct the gods.

3. Through Agni may we riches gain,
And day by day prosperity
Replete with fame and manly sons.

4. The worship and the sacrifice,
Guarded by thee on every side,
Go straight, O Agni, to the gods.

5. May Agni, the invoker, wise
And true, of most resplendent fame,
The god, come hither with the gods.

6. Whatever good thou wilt bestow,
O Agni, on the pious man,
That gift comes true, O Angiras.

7. To thee, O Agni, day by day,
O thou illuminer of gloom,
With thought we, bearing homage, come:

8. To thee the lord of sacrifice,
The radiant guardian of the Law,
That growest in thine own abode.

9. So, like a father to his son,
Be easy of approach to us;
Agni, for weal abide with us.

I, 143. METRE: JAGATI; 8 TRISTUBH.

1. A mightier, newer hymn to Agni I present;
My words and song to him, the son of strength,
I bring,
Who, offspring of the waters, with bright gods sat down,
As regular and dear invoker, on the earth.

2. As soon as he was in the highest heaven born,
To Matarisvan Agni manifest became;
As he was kindled, by his might and majesty
His brilliant light illuminated Heaven and Earth.

3. His flames that grow not old, the beams of Agni's fire,
Whose aspect, countenance, and sheen are beautiful,
With mighty radiance undulate and shine afar,
Like glistening rivers' flow: they slumber not nor age.

4. The god, all-knowing Agni, whom the Bhrgus brought
With might to earth's navel, the centre of the world.
Him stimulate with songs within his own abode,
Who rules, sole sovereign, over wealth, like Varuna.

5. Who like the Maruts' roar, or like a dart discharged,
Or like the heavenly bolt can never be restrained:
Agni, the god, with pointed fangs consumes and chews;
He, as a warrior his foes, lays low the woods.

6. Will Agni be a glad receiver of our praise?
Will he, the bright one, with bright goods grant our desire?
Will he incite, inspire our thoughts to gain their ends?
Him of the radiant face now with this song I laud.

7. Who kindles Agni, butter-faced, that draws aloft
Your sacrifice, he strives to win him as a friend.
When kindled as a shining banner at our rites,
May he uplift our radiant-coloured hymn of praise.

8. Incessantly with guards unceasing, Agni,
That are auspicious and strong, protect us.
With guards that slumber not, unfailing, watchful,
Preserve, O helper, all our children safely.

VI, 6. METRE: TRISTUBH.

1. The man who seeks success and aid approaches
The son of strength, with feast and newest worship.
He rends the wood and has a blackened pathway,
The brightly radiant and divine invoker.

2. The shining thunderer who dwells in lustre,
With his unaging, roaring flames, most youthful,
Refulgent Agni, frequently recurring,
Goes after many spacious woods and chews them.

3. Thy flames when driven by the wind, O Agni,
Disperse, O pure one, pure in all directions;
And thy divine Navagvas, most destructive,
Lay low the woods and devastate them boldly.

4. Thy steeds, the bright, the pure, O radiant Agni,
Let loose speed on and shave the ground beneath them.

Thy whirling flame then widely shines refulgent,
The highest ridges of earth's surface reaching.

5. When the bull's tongue darts forward like the missile
Discharged by him who fights the cows to capture,
Like hero's onset is the flame of Agni:
Resistless, dreadful, he consumes the forests.

6. Thou with the sunbeams of the great impeller,
Hast boldly overspread the earthly spaces.
So with thy mighty powers drive off all terrors;
Attack our rivals and burn down our foemen.

7. Give us, O splendid one of splendid lordship,
Wealth giving splendour, splendid, life-imparting.
Bestow bright wealth and vast with many heroes,
Bright god, with thy bright flames, upon the singer.

SOMA

As the Soma sacrifice forms the centre of the ritual of the Rigveda, this is one of the most prominent deities, coming next in importance to Agni, as indicated by the number of hymns addressed to him. His anthropomorphism is little developed, because the plant and its juice are constantly present to the mind and the vision of the poet.

Soma has sharp and terrible weapons, which he grasps in his hand; he wields a bow and a thousand-pointed shaft. He has a celestial car drawn by a team like Vayu's; he is also said to ride on the same car as Indra; and he is the best of charioteers. He is associated as a dual divinity in about half a dozen hymns with Indra, Agni, Ptisan and Rudra. He is sometimes attended by the Maruts, Indra's close allies. He comes to the sacrifice to receive the offerings, and seats himself on the sacred grass. The intoxicating Soma juice is often called "mead" (mad/iu), but more often the "drop" (indu). Its colour is brown, ruddy, or more usually tawny. The whole of the ninth book of the Rigveda consists of incantations chanted over the tangible Soma, while its stalks are being pounded by the pressing stones, and the juice, passing through the strainer of sheep's wool, flows into wooden vats, in which it is offered to the gods on the sacred grass. These processes are overlaid with confused and mystical imagery, endlessly varied.

The filtered Soma is mixed with water as well as milk, by which it is sweetened. Soma's connexion with the waters is expressed in many ways. He is the drop that grows in the waters; he is the embryo of the waters or their child; they are his mothers or his sisters; he is lord and king of streams; he produces waters and causes heaven and earth to rain. The sound of the flowing juice is often expressed by verbs meaning to roar, bellow, or even thunder. He is therefore frequently called a bull among the cows (representing the waters). He is, moreover, swift, being often compared with a steed, sometimes with a bird flying to the wood. His yellow colour suggests his brilliance, the physical aspect of Soma on which the poets dwell most frequently. He is then often compared with or associated with the sun.

The exhilarating effect of Soma caused it to be regarded as a drink bestowing immortal life, and to be called the draught of immortality (amrta}. All the gods drink Soma; they drank it to gain immortality; it confers immortality not only on the gods, but on men. It also has healing powers, making the blind to see and the lame to walk. As stimulating the voice, Soma is called "Lord of Speech." He awakens eager thought: he is a generator of hymns, a leader of poets, a seer among priests. His wisdom is hence much dwelt on: he is a wise seer, and knows the races of the gods.

The exhilarating powers of Soma are most emphasized in connection with Indra, whom it stimulates for the fight with Vrtra in innumerable ways. Through this association Indra's warlike exploits come to be attributed to Soma himself: he is a victor unconquered in fight, born for battle; as a warrior he wins all kinds of wealth for his worshippers.

Soma is in several passages said to grow or dwell on the mountains, but his true origin and abode are thought to be in heaven. Soma is the child of heaven, is the milk of heaven, and is purified in heaven; he is the lord of heaven; he occupies heaven, and his place is the highest heaven, Thence he was brought to earth: the myth embodying this belief is that of the eagle that brings Soma to Indra. Being the most important of herbs, Soma is said to have been born as the lord of plants, whose king he is; he is the lord of the wood, and has generated all plants. In a few of the latest hymns of the Rigveda Soma begins to be mystically identified with the moon ; in the Atharvaveda Soma several times means the moon ; and in the Brahmanas this identification has already become a commonplace.

The preparation and the offering of Soma (the Avestan Haoma) were already an important feature in Indo-Iranian worship. In both the Rigveda and the Avesta it is said that the Soma stalks were pressed, that its juice was yellow, and was mixed with milk; in both Soma grows on the mountains, though its mythical home is in heaven, whence it comes down to earth; in both Soma has become a mighty god and is called a king ; in both there are many other identical mythological traits. It is possible that the belief in an intoxicating divine beverage, the home of which was in heaven, goes back to the Indo-European period; if so, it must have been regarded as a kind of honey-mead (Sanskrit mddhu, Greek /xe'tfv, Anglo-Saxon medu}. The name of Soma means "pressed juice," being derived from su (avestan 7z), "to press." The following hymn does not touch upon the processes of the production of Soma, but dwells on the inspiring, life-giving, remedial, protective, and beneficial powers of the god.

VIII, 48. METRE: TRISTUBH ; 5 JAGATI.

1. I have partaken wisely of the sweet food

That stirs good thoughts, best banisher of trouble,

The food round which all deities and mortals.

Calling it honey-mead, collect together,

2. Thou shalt be Aditi when thou hast entered

Within, appeaser of celestial anger.

May'st thou, O drop, enjoying Indra's friendship,

Like willing mare the car, to wealth advance us.

3. We have drunk Soma and become immortal;
We have attained the light the gods discovered.
What can hostility now do against us?
And what, immortal god, the spite of mortals?

4. Be cheering to our heart when drunk, O Indu,
Kindly, like father to his son, O Soma.
Like friend for friend, far-famed one, wisely
Prolong our years that we may live, O Soma.

5. These glorious, freedom-giving drops, when drunk by me,
Have knit my joints together as do thongs a car.
May these protect me now from fracturing a limb.
And may they ever keep me from disease remote.

YAJUR VEDA

INTRODUCTION

Genesis of the Vedas.

Vedas are the Word of God, revealed in the beginning of creation for the moral, spiritual and physical guidance and uplift of humanity. They are replete with eternal truths and throw a flood of light on the various aspects of life to make a man perfect and ideal. God out of His infinite source of knowledge reveals in the beginning of creation a part of it adequate for the requirements of the soul, its spiritual satisfaction, fulfilment of its thirst for truth and making its journey of life successful.

God is infinite, the soul is finite. The finite soul cannot contain the infinite knowledge of God, God creates, sustains and dissolves the world. Whenever the world is created God reveals the Vedas. These processes going on since eternity and will go on for ever. Maharshi Patanjali writes in the Mahabhashya, that there are 101 Shakhas (schools of thought) of the Yajurveda. All of these commentaries are not available at present except the Kanva, Madhyandini, Taitriya, Maitrayani, Kathak, and Kapishthal. On this point Maharshi Dayananda agrees with Patanjali. There was a time when the learned Pundits memorised one or more Vedas, could recite or reproduce them from memory, but alas this system is no longer in vogue due to lack of public and state patronage. The names of the Rishis attached to the Mantras are the names o0066 those research scholars and seers, who expounded the meanings of the verses and commented upon them. They are not the authors or writers of those verses as the western scholars say. Devata is the subject matter of a verse, the topic discussed in it. All good men and beneficent forces of nature like air, fire, water, electricity, months, sun, moon, breaths, lightning, father, mother, teacher, preacher, and soul, which are beneficial to humanity are called devatas. They are not all living, personified beings as some erroneously believe them to be.

CHAPTER I

1. O, Lord, we resort to Thee for the supply of foodstuffs and vigour. May the Creator, the fountain of happiness and knowledge, inspire us for the performance of noblest deeds with our organs. May the cows, which should never be killed, be healthy and strong. For the attainment of prosperity and wealth, may the cows be full of calves, free from consumption and other diseases. Maya thief and a sinner be never born amongst us. May the lord of land and cattle be in constant and full possession of these. May Ye protect the cattle, wealth and progeny of the virtuous soul.

2. Yajna acts as purifier, makes explicit, true and perfect knowledge, spread in space through the rays of the sun, purifies the air, is the mainstay of the universe, and also adds to our comfort through its exalted office. It behoves us all the learned and their followers not to give up the performance of yajnas.

3. The yajna of the Great Lord is the supporter of innumerable worlds and purifies us all. May the Self-Effulgent Lord, lead us aright on the path of virtue. May He purify us through the store of true knowledge and all sciences contained in the Vedas, and elevating selfless deeds. O ye men which branches of true knowledge do ye want to comprehend ?

4. Vedas are the true source of knowledge and their study enables us to enjoy the full span of life. They contain the detailed instructions concerning various duties. May we through His grace be firmly con- vinced of the utility of industrial achievements, and may He, the Omnipresent Lord protect our yajnas and the knowledge and means thereof.

5. O God, the Lord of Vows, I will observe the vow. May I have strength for that. Pray grant me success in the fulfilment of my vow. I take the vow of renouncing untruth and embracing truth.

6. Who prompts you to do good deeds ? It is He, the Great Lord Who guides us on the path of virtue. Why does He do so ? For the performance of noble, virtuous deeds and the fulfilment of the vow of leading a truthful life. The Lord enjoins the workers and their organisers, the teacher and the taught to be constantly engaged in doing good deeds and achieving fine qualities and true knowledge,

7- May we root out the evil tendencies of the wicked, the unsym- pathetic and uncharitable exploiters of humanity. May we take to task the disturbers of peace, and expose the wicked. May we thus get many an opportunity of attaining to prosperity and bliss.

8. O Lord, Thou art the dispeller of vices. May Thou punish - the wicked. May Thou deal with the vicious that put the sages to trouble. May Thou inspire the sinful with noble thought, whom we, too, exhort to do noble deeds. We worship

Thee, the Giver of happiness and knowledge to the learned, purifier of them, the Promulgator of learning and joy in the universe, and worthy of adoration by the religious minded devotees and the wise.

9. O Ye men, increase the store of goods acquired by honest and fair means to be used in the service of humanity. May your life, be constantly dedicated to this principle. May the spiritually minded people, also, not give up this humanitarian work. May your lives be constantly consecrated to the performance of five daily duties. The heat of the sun destroys dirt and odour, and draws substances consigned to fire, in their atomic form for the purification of air.

10. In this universe created by the All Effulgent God, I realize the power and influence of the sun and moon, feel the inhalation and exhalation of life-giving breath, appreciate the efforts made by the votaries of knowledge for mastering science of electricity. I follow the researches made by the learned in the applications of water and fire.

11. I resort to agriculture and craft for removing poverty and ministering happiness to all. May I feel joy in my domestic life. May our houses be sufficiently commodious, airy, fully comfortable, and built in the middle of an open space. May our life be in conformity with Vedic teachings. O Lord we pray unto Thee to preserve and protect whatever gives us happiness.

12. O learned persons, just as in this world created by God, inhal- ing and exhaling breaths are purified by the faultless and pure rays of the sun, just as charming and beautiful waters, which run to the ocean and go up in the atmosphere and nourish medicines are purified by these rays, so do ye perform Homa with pure substances. I always promote this yajna, and sanctify the worshipper with pure mind and strong body, the worshipper full of learning and noble qualities.

13. O performers of yajnas, as the sun receives the aforesaid waters and the air to dispel clouds, and absorbs them for the fast moving clouds, hence ye should always perform yajnas.

We all should perform agreeable yajnas, for the attainment of God, for noble acts, for the acquisition of fine virtues and for temporal and spiritual advancement. With the aid of yajnas purify all substances and human beings. Yajnas will remove all your physical and mental defects. I, the Revealer of the Veda, advance this purificatory act of yours.

14. May your house be comfortable. It should afford no shelter to the wicked and the uncharitable. May your house serve on as skin of the Earth. May all persons acquire such a house through the grace of God. Clouds receive moisture from forests, reside in the vast space, and receive water from air. May God impart you this knowledge of clouds and building houses. May the learned understand the building of houses, which serve as skin of the earth.

15. O yajna, thou art the body of the fire. Thou art performed with the recitation of

vedic verses, I perform thee for the acquisition of noble qualities. Thou art a great cloud, the fosterer of herbs, Cleanse this oblation, the assuager of mental pain, for the happiness of the learned Cleanse it well. Those who read and teach the Vedas, become acquainted with the Vedic lore, inspiring us for the performance of yajnas.

16. The yajna keeps away the thieves, refines and sweetens the speech, is productive of foodstuffs and is the bestower of knowledge and vigour. Let the performance of such yajnas be inculcated. May we through the aid of heroic persons win battles again and again. The yajna is instrumental in producing rain, may we know thee as rain producer. We should try to efface the dacoits and exploiters of impure minds who lead an impious life.

Just as the air with its strong hands of definite motion to and fro receives the oblations and just as the bright Sun full of luminous beams, with his faultless rays resolves into atoms the substances put into the fire, so do God and the scholars preach all sciences for the good of humanity.

17. O Lord, dauntless art Thou. Let us avoid in a yajna the use of fire that burns the corpses, and use the fire, that ripens the raw com- modities, and endows us with nobler qualities. Through thy teachings re- move our miseries and confer bliss on us.

13. I refers to God.

14. Just as skin protects and beautifies the body, so should our houses beautify the plot on which they are built.

Lord, Thou art the bestower of permanent happiness. May the Earth and the beings living on it advance through high merits. We re- alise in our hearts for the removal of the wicked, Thee who bestoweth happiness upon the learned, the heroic and all sentient beings.

18. O 1 Lord, Thou art the sustainer of the universe. Accept our adoration offered through Vedic verses and develop our inexhaustible mental knowledge. For the destruction of internal foes I realise Thee in my heart as the Supporter of the learned, the statesman and the Guide on the path of duty of different classes. Thou art the Supporter of the un- iverse, we pray unto Thee to increase our knowledge. For the destruc- tion of our internal foes, we realise Thee in our hearts as the Supporter of the learned, the statesman and the Guide on the path of duty of different classes. I imbibe in my heart Thee the All pervader, the Giver of happi- ness from all directions.

O Ye men, lead a life of penance by controlling your breath, and following the wise, the scientists and the learned.

19. The yajna is the giver of happiness, puts an end to the selfish and miserly habits and protects the mid-regions as skin protects the body. May the performer

of the yajna realise its significance. The proper reci- tation of the vedic hymns is the yajna in itself. The yajna performed on special occasions also protects the truth as skin protects the body. The yajna is the sustainer of the illustrious sun, the embodiment of Vedic lore. May we realise the yajna as the bringer of rain, and the giver of spiritual knowledge.

20. The foodstuffs and water purified by the performance of yajna strengthen the body and sense organs. May we resort to yajna for sound health, for activities, for vitality, for long life full of happiness and pro- sperity. The glorious Creator and Emancipator of the universe, through His perfect Omnipresence, blesses us for the dissemination of true sublime knowledge.

21. O men, just as I the Lord, propagate the knowledge of this yajna in the world created by Me, and perform it through the bright sun, stable Earth, vitalizing air and various kinds of breaths in the human organism, so do ye. May you prepare, for your benefit, mixtures of different medicines with water and with juices and dilute the same again with distilled water. May you, thus, effect useful combinations of the beneficial medicines, with refined tinctures.

22. I fully harness the yajna for the attainment of happiness and material prosperity. This oblation is put into the fire, which expands, reaches in the middle region of the sun and moon and produces food-stuff. The yajna confers fuller life and happiness. May this yajna be pef fotmed everywhere. May the performer of the yajna spread its knowledge. May the sacrificial Agni keep us free from diseases. May the indwelling Effulgent God, make our yajna perfect for the attainment of complete joys.

23. Be fearless and do not waver as to the performance of yajna. Let the offspring of the performer of this yajna be excellent, faithful and free from weakness. We whole heartedly take recourse to yajnas for the realisation of the one Lord, for the purification of air and water and for getting the blessings of mother, father and preceptor.

24. By the impulse of God the Giver of bliss, I perform the yajna free from Hinsa (violence), for the attainment of noble qualities and association of the learned, through the aid of life-giving-breath, vitalising air, and through the rejuvenating rays of the sun and moon. A yajna is the recipient of the rays of the sun that ripens a large variety of objects and is full of immense lustre, and innumerable rays. A yajna is the illuminating source of rain. With the aid of the yajna we should remove our miseries.

25. O God, the Creator of the solar and bright regions we implore Thee that through Thy grace, may we not destroy the medicinal herbs of the earth, on which the learned perform the yajnas. May the yajna reach the clouds. Let the sun pour rain on the earth through its rays. O heroic persons bind by various fetters a wicked man in this world, who is opposed to us and is opposed to by us, and release him not.

26. O' Omnipresent Lord, the Giver of happiness, may we subjugate the wicked folk on this earth where the sages perform yajnas. May we associate with the learned and, thus spread freely the system of education as propounded in the Vedic hymns. Just as My light of knowledge is valued by all, so should yours. The ignorant moving in the dark who are opposed to the learned, and whom the learned disapprove for their antagonism to knowledge, should be brought round to the path of virtue by hundreds of means available and let the restriction on them be not removed till their enlightenment. May the wicked, be not blessed with prosperity, and the pleasure of knowledge. O Ye dutiful may ye persistently follow the path of virtue.

27. I perform the yajna with the recitation of vedic verses in Gayatri, Trishtup, and Jagati metres. O Earth, thou art beautiful, a source of prosperity, and happiness, a fit place to dwell upon comfortably, full of corn, milk, sweet juices and fruits.

28. O Almighty Lord Tbpu, hast suspended in space near Moon, this Earth, full of foodstuffs, and producer of all the life-giving substances for the living creatures. May the learned of refined intellect, full of happiness, residing upon it, the well-wisher of all. abiding by Thy eternal laws, conquer all foes waging severe fight with the aid of warriors and arms, thus attain to power. O learned person, just as from times immemorial the dutiful have been acquiring wealth, so do thou full of wealth worship God. Let evil be eradicated.

29. The wicked should be removed, the enemies of truth should be punished ; those fit to be shackled should be cast aside and those opposed to knowledge should come to grief. Oh destroyer of foes, Thou art not wrathful, I prepare thee full of virility for battle.

Those who can't tolerate the good of others must be chastised, and openly condemned. Those who cause harm to others should be humiliated. I duly instruct the army to be strong for weakening the foe, and waging war.

30. O 1 Lord Thou art the Creator of juices in the soil. Thou art the Omnipresent, the Pervader of all. Like the flame of fire Thou art in- extinguishable. Thou art worthy of worship by the sages at all places, meant for it, through the recitation of the vedic texts. May we realise Thee through our peaceful spiritual vision, for our advancement.

31. I consecrate the yajna, which purifies all objects with the

32. According to some interpreters, Gayatri chhand is synonymous with a Brahman* Trishtup with a Kshatriya, and Jagati with a Vaishya. Some interpret these verses as earth, mid-region, and sun. Some interpret Gayatri as fire, Trishtup as air, and Jagati as sun. Some interpret them as head, chest and loins, some as Vasu, Rudra and Aditya, and some as Pran, Apan and Vyan. In prosody Gayatri metre consists of 24, Tnshtup of 44 & Jagati of 48 syllables just as a Vasu Brahmchari observes celibacy for 24 years, a Rudra for 44, and an Aditya for 48 years.

33. YAJUR VEDA flawless, pure rays of the sun. In this world created by the Great Lord, I sanctify the hearts and souls of the people by the pure and ever soul-illuminating knowledge. O' Lord Thou art the source of all light, Pure, Giver of the bliss of emancipation, the final resort of the universe ; fit to be adored by the learned, loved by the sincere, fearless devotees, Invincible and worshipped by the sages.

CHAPTER II

1. Oh yajna, thou art being performed in a well dug place, them art i?refied by fire and attracted by the air. For the sake of Havan I consecrate the oblation agreeably rectified by thee. Thou art an alter for taking the oblations high up into the space ; I erect thee and con- secrate thee with ghee. Just jasjyater in the space contributes to the purification of the material objects, so do I carefully cleanse the oblations to be put into the fire ladles.

2. Yajna showers water on the Earth. Mortar is the chief receptacle of the yajna. I prepare the altar for the learned to sit on. May those scholars sing the praises of God, the Earth's Lord, the World's Lord, the Lord of Kings.

3. The jsun^ sustainer of the world and the holder of the earth, spreads the yajna far and wide for the happiness of the universe. Adorable fire, being adored in the yajna, thou art the guardian of the worshipper. O yajna thou art the induce r of rain through the power of sun for the happiness of the universe. Adorable fire, being adored in the yajna, thou art the guardian of the worshipper. Inhalation and exhalation, for the happiness of the universe, protect thee (yajna) with firm strength every now and then. Adorable fire, being adored in the yajna, thou art the protector of the worshipper.

4. May we, in a friendly spirit, manifest Thy glory Oh Omniscient, All-illumining God, the Giver of great happiness to all, the Embodiment of effulgence, and the Preacher of the yajnas.

5. Oh yajna, Thou art beautiful like the spring. The sun protects thee from time immemorial, for unfolding all objects. Thou art diffused through the power and potency (the two arms) of the sun. Just as Vasus, Rudras, and Adityas promote the yajna, the giver of happiness, pervaded in space, so do I for the acquisition of divine qualities, perform the yajna.

6. Oh Yajna, thy name is sky, thou art full of butter, be confirmed in this decorated place with thy lovely glory. Oh Yajna thy name is space, thou art full of water, be confirmed in this decorated space with thy lovely glory. Oh Yajna thy name is Earth, thou art the giver of longevity, be confirmed in this decorated place with thy lovely glory. May necessary articles be placed in the holy yajna. O God, may Thou protect those articles, may Thou protect the Yajna, may Thou protect the worshipper, may Thou protect me the conductor of the Yajna.

7. I kindle the fire, the giver of corn, full of intensity, the carrier of all oblations to the sky, and the bringer of victory in war. The fire properly used in the Yajna brings water through the forces of nature,

8. May I today for the acquisition of comforts collect through Yajna butter and other articles which contribute to happiness.

O God may I never violate it (Yajna). O Lord may I obtain Thy refuge, abounding in store of riches. This fire is the abode of yajna. Through it (yajna) sun and air gain strength. This yajna resides in space and fire.

9. Oh God protect the sun and earth, which protect the yajna. Just as fire acquiring the yajna and acting as an envoy, protects the sun and earth, so protect us, Oh Lord the doer of the noble deeds for the learned. Just as the sun combining light with light through the oblations put into fire, protects the heaven and earth so God guard us with the light of spiritual knowledge. This is thus ordained in the Veda.

10. May God bestow on me spiritual power. May we obtain wealth full of various kinds of splendour, and earthly power. May our desires be fulfilled, may they attain to fruition, Men use this Earth and knowledge (whereby salvation is attained) for the pleasures of kingship. May these Earth and knowledge advise me. May God, as my last Refuge and resort instruct me. This is thus ordained in the Veda.

11. I have prayed to the Effulgent, All sustaining God, May the Lord Father accept my prayer. Our digestive faculty digests by means of gastric juice the food put into the stomach. In this universe created by the All-Blissful God, I take that food through the qualities of attraction and retention, of inhalation and exhalation ; and the forces of purification and permeation of the invigorating air, throughout the body. Cooking my food in the burnt fire I eat it with my mouth.

12. Oh Lord the Creator of the universe, the Vedas and the learned proclaim this fore-mentioned yajna of Thine for Brihaspati and Brahma. Through that great sacrifice protect my yajna, protect the performer of the yajna, protect Thou me.

13. May my active mind enjoy the yajna's provisions. May God expand and preserve this unabandonable acquisition of knowledge, which is a kind of yajna. May all the learned persons in the world rejoice. May Om be seated in our hearts.

14. Oh God, may Thou be glorified by our praises sung through Thy Vedas. May Thou promote our knowledge. Oh God, may we advance our soul. O God Thou controllest the activities of all. Thou art the embodiment of knowledge. Thou art Omniscient and the Bringer of victory in battles. May we prosper and sing Thy praises. I become pure and holy by following Thy commands.

15. May I achieve victory like the victory of Fire and Moon. May I speed onward with the materials of war. May Fire and Moon, drive off him who hates us, drive off the man whom we detest. May I remove that sinful enemy by warlike, military skill and equipment. May I achieve victory like the victory of Air and Lightning. May I achieve happiness through the impulse of knowledge, used for the acquisition of supremacy. May air and lightning properly employed, drive off him who hates us, drive of the man whom we dislike. I purify this ignorant person by the light of knowledge.

16. We perform the yajna for Vasus, Rudras and Adityas. The light of the sun and

earth bring thee (yajna) to light. The Pran (external air) and Udan (internal air) protect thee through rain. Just as birds go to their nests, so let us daily go to the yajna reciting Gayatri Mantras.

17. Oh Omnipresent God, extolled by the praises of the learned, Thou attainest to greatness through those lovely panegyrics. I realise that greatness of Thine in my heart. May I never disobey Thee. May I, Oh God, never abuse the pleasant and invigorating food, I have secured in Thy creation.

18. May ye thriving, justice loving, wise, learned persons, preachers of the knowledge of the Vedas, become supreme through knowledge. Let all seekers after truth, devotees of learning and action, attain to happiness. Preach My noble word, that brings all kinds of joys.

19. Oh fire and air, ye are the bringers of rain. Ye protect the yajna, and conduce to our comfort, bring comfort to me. God and humi- lity are near me for my good, as they are for thine. Just as I derive happiness by the performance of yajna, so should you.

20. Oh Immortal, Omnipresent God, protect me from intense pain, protect me from the bondages of sin and ignorance, protect me from the company of evil-minded persons, protect me from food injurious to health. Make Thou our food free from poison. Let me live in a comfortable house; praying to Thee and doing noble needs. This is our prayer to the Lord of the Universe, may we get pure knowledge through the vedas, the givers of glory and prosperity.

21. Oh God, Thou knowest the animate and the inanimate creation. Thou knowest everything in the universe. Just as Thou art the expo- under of knowledge for the learned, so dost Thou expound knowledge unto me. Ye learned people, who know how to sing praises unto God, knowing the veda that shows the right path, should master knowledge. Oh God, the Master of learning, rightfully fix this yajnalike world in the air.

22. May the mighty space unite with oblation and butter. May it unite with the twelve months of the year, and eight lifegiving age- ncies and vital breaths, May the sun be harnessed with all its rays. May pure water rain whenever duly consecrated oblations are offered.

23. Does anybody abandon the sacrifice? He who abandons it, is abandoned by God. For what purpose does the worshipper put the oblations into the fire ? He does it for the happiness of all. He does it for gaining strength, health and vigour. The inferior articles not used in the sacrifice are the allotted portion of the fiends.

24. May we be endowed with the study of the Vedas, knowledge, stout bodies, peaceful and devoted minds. May God, the Giver of happi- ness grant us riches, and banish each blemish from our body.

25. The Yajna performed by us in Jagati metre goes up to the sky. From there it

is sent back and pleases the world. By means of this Yajna, may we ward off the man who hates us, and him whom we detest.

The yajna performed by us in Trishtup metre goes up in the air. From there it is released and affords happiness to the world by the purification of air and water. By means of this yajna, we keep away the man who hates us, and him whom we dislike. The yajna performed by us in Gayatri metre spreads on the Earth, and being released from there goes up to heaven, and purifies the objects of the Earth. By means of this yajna we remove the man who hates us, and him whom we despise. By the use of food purified through yajna, may we get happiness, for the accomplishment of the yajna, and be combined with lustre.

26. Oh God Thou art Self-Existent, Most Excellent, and Self Effulgent, Giver art thou of knowledge. Give me knowledge. I follow the command of God.

27. Oh Lord of the universe, Oh God, may I become a good householder through Thee, the protector of the universe. Oh Lord may Thou protect my house, being adored by me the guardian of my house. May our domestic duties be performed free from idleness. May I live for a hundred years day and night in the presence of God.

28. Oh God, the Lord of vows, pray grant me success in the performance of the vows, which I have undertaken, and which I find myself confident to discharge. I reap as I sow.

29. Speak reverentially to the learned, the repository of know- ledge. Speak sweetly and gently to your father, mother, teacher and the Brahmchari. Exterminate all fiends and evil-minded persons in the world.

30. Oh God remove from this world the demoniacal beings who walk on the earth, dissembling their real intentions, who are immersed in the attainment of their selfish aims, and are filled with evil ambitions.

31. In this world, let the wise and the learned enjoy, let them be strong, healthy and pleased, according to their capacity. Let them be happy, hale and hearty according to their resources.

32. Obeisance unto Yee, O Fathers, for the acquisition of happi- ness and knowledge. Obeisance unto Yee, O Fathers for the removal of misery and enemies. Obeisance unto Yee, O Fathers for longevity, Obeisance unto Yee, O Fathers, for sovereignty, and display of justice. Obeisance unto Yee, O Fathers, for the cessation of manifold calamities,

33. Accept thou teacher, in the womb of thy discipleship, the youth, with a garland of flowers in hand, eager for knowledge, so that he may attain to full manhood.

34. Oh sons, please my parents and teachers by offering them various juices, sweet waters, disease-dissipating articles, milk, clarified butter, well-cooked food, and juicy fruits. Enjoy your own wealth, and covet not the wealth of others.

CHAPTER III

1. Oh learned persons, kindle the fire with the wood sticks, with butter, set ablaze the fire, which is worthy of respect like a Sanyasi. Put oblations in this fire of the yajna.

2. Put the oblations of ghee that removes physical infirmities, into this well ablaze, disease-killing fire present in all objects.

3. We fan with sticks of wood and ghee the fire, that is powerful in splitting all things, and burns intensely.

4. O beautiful fire, wood sticks soaked with ghee go unto thee along with oblations. May thou accept my fuel put into thee.

5. I lay upon the back of the Earth upon which the learned per- form yajna, which is like Heaven in plenty, and like Earth in grandeur, for gain of eatable food, this food-eating fire, that pervades the Earth, Ether, and Sky.

6. This Earth revolves in the L. space, _jt revolves with its mother water in its orbit. It inc^ej^oun^t^fatherTlEc^TiL

7. The lustre of this fire, goes up and comes down in the space like exhalation and inhalation in the body. This great fire displays the Sun.

8. God's word rules supreme throughout the world. The Vedas arc recited for acquiring the knowledge of God. We should resolutely recite and understand the Vedas everyday with their illuminating sayings.

9. Just as God gives the light of truthful speech to all human beings, so does physical fire give light that illumines all substances. Just as God inculcates knowledge in the souls of all, that man should speak, as he feels in his heart, so does the Sun bring to light all physical objects. Just as God reveals for humanity all the four Vedas, the store- house of knowledge, so doesJSreJn_thc_shape_ ofjlightning^^exist in the space, and become the source of rain and knowledge.

Just as God, through the Vedas displays all sciences, fire, and lightning, so does the Sun develop our physical and spiritual forces. Sun illumines all objects. God is self-Resplendent. This is the manifestation of His Glory.

10. This enjoyable fire, in accompaniment with the recital of Vcdic texts, mixed with God's creation and dark night, with flashes of lightning pervades all objects.

This sun, mixed with God's creation and brilliant dawn, receives the oblations put into the fire, and carries them to places far and wide.

11. Performing sacrifice, may we pronounce vedic texts, in praise of God, who hears us from far and near.

12. Men should worship God alone, who is the Great and Supreme Lord, who sustains the luminous Sun, and the non-luminous Earth, who knows the formation of the vitality of waters.

13. Oh Electricity and Fire, I invoke Ye both for knowing your attributes, for enjoying the pleasures of riches. Ye both are the givers of desired sovereignty. Ye twain I invoke for consuming excellent food.

14. Oh God, in Thy creation, sacrificial fire, whose cause of birth is air, burns in different seasons, and develops in all directions. Knowing this, cause our riches increase.

15. In this world the instructors and the learned kindle in serviceable yajnas, for mankind, the ubiquitous fire of extra-ordinary qualities.

That fire is recognised by the regulators of sacrifice as worthy of adoration, as the first means of the performance of a yajna, as the receiver of sacrifice aad giver of happiness and scientific knowledge.

16. The learned, knowing the eternity, lustre, thousandfold service, and usefulness of fire, get pure water from it.

17. Thou. God, art our bodies 1 protector. Protect Thou, my body.

Giver of longevity art Thou, O God, Give me longevity. Giver of splendour art Thou, O God, Give me splendour. Remove, O God, all the defects of my body and soul.

18. Oh God, the Lord of manifold riches, may we, being free from pride, enjoying long life, and practising forbearance, live for a hundred years, praising Thee the Effulgent, the Eternal, the Forbearing, the Un- conquerable, and the Killer of foes.

Through Thy kindness, being free from woes, may we attain to happiness.

19. Oh God, thou art full of splendour like the Sun, sung by the sages with vedic verses, and O Thou full of power for protection May I attain to long life, to splendour, to offspring, and abundant riches.

20. May I enjoy the life-bestowing food through the plants and medicines that contribute to health and vigour. May I utilise the science of air and water for the accomplishment of my deeds. May I get the essence of food from milk, honey and fruits. May I enjoy the abundance of good articles through objects full of manifold qualities.

21. Oh Vedic speech, may thou remain in this altar in this yajnd, in this spot and in this house. Remain here, and go not far from hence.

22. Oh universal vedic text, thou art full of vigour and valour, may we attain unto thee, the master of the yajna. O God, may we be in communion with Thee, everyday, morning and evening, bowing unto Thee through our intellect.

23. May we worship God, who is the Guardian of sacrifices, Radiant, the Revealer of the vedas, and attained to complete redemption.

24. Oh God, Thou givest unto us knowledge, as a father to his son. Unite us perpetually with pleasure.

25. Oh God, Thou art the Bestower on us of ears to hear goodness, the Shelter of mankind, the Embodiment of the lustre of knowledge, and real Omnipresence. Thou pervadest our soul. Thou art our Protector, Our Benefactor, and possessest excellent nature, attributes and deeds. Give us wealth most splendidly renowned.

26. O most pure, O radiant God, verily do we pray to Thee for the happiness of our friends. Give us knowledge, listen to our praises and prayers, and keep us far from every evil.

27. O God, may I get land for ruling over it, may I be endowed with statesmanship. May noble desires reside in me. May I be the centre of the fulfilment of all ambitions.

28. O God, the Guardian of the primordial vedas, make me, like the son of a learned person, endowed with different capacities for the acquisi- tion of knowledge, an imparter of instruction, and a fulfiller of the aim of education.

29. God is rich and the dispeller of ignorance. He knows the true nature of all things, and grants us physical and spiritual strength. He is prompt. May he goad us to noble deeds.

30. O God, may not our knowledge of the Vedas ever perish. May Thou preserve us from the violence of the uncharitable person.

31. God, may we get the great, wise and unassailable protection of the three forces of nature, the water, the sun and the air.

32. Those who worship God are not molested by evil-minded foes neither at home, nor upon pathways and battlefields. I become capable of acquiring God and the sages.

33. They, the sons of indestructible matter, bestow eternal light upon man for his life and death.

34. O God, Thou art the giver of happiness. If Thou dost not bestow knowledge promptly on a charitable person, he again, O Liberal Lord, does not attain to Thy bounty.

35. O Creator of the Universe I O All holy and worthy of adoration ! May we

meditate on Thy adorable self. May Thou guide our understanding.

36. Oh God, may Thine immortal knowledge, wherewith Thou guardest the learned in all directions, come close from all sides.

37. O God, friendly to the wise, do Thou protect my offspring. O worthy of praise do Thou protect my cattle. O God, above all suspicion, protect my food. O God, through Thy grace, in unison with the three life-winds, Pran, Apan and Vyan, may I be rich in offspring, well-manned with men, a hero with the heroes, and strong with wise and invigorating deeds.

38. O, Ocean of Light, the Omniscient, the best knower of all the worlds, and enjoyments may we well approach Thee. May Thou spread for us splendour and strength in all directions.

39. Lord of our houses, O God, Thou art the best finder of riches for our children, Thou art the protector of our hearths, and the com- panion of the householders. Bestow splendour and strength on us.

40. This fire assists us in the accomplishment of our deeds. It is rich, and furtherer of plenty. O God, the Giver of our comforts, bestow splendour and strength upon us.

41. Fear not, nor tremble Ye, O householders. We, bearing strength, come to Ye. May I bearing strength, intelligent and happy, rejoicing in my mind, enjoy all pleasures and approach the householders.

42. We praise the householders, whom the guest staying far from home remembers and whom he loves much. The loving householders welcome us, the religious guests.

43. May we in this world get cows, goats, sheep and abundant food in our houses. I come to you for safety and quietude, May I acquire mundane and celestial joy and felicity.

44. We invocate the guests, who are delightful, free from ignorance, removers of sins, eaters of the food well cooked, and full of knowledge.

45. May we forsake each sinful act that we have committed in village or solitude, in an assembly or corporeal sense. Let every man so resolve.

46. O God, protect us in battles, in this world, with the help of heroes and destroy us not. O mighty hero, verily, as the vedic voice, re-

47. They, who with delightful vedic voice, working in cooperation, perform their desired deeds, go to their comfortable house, after the com- pletion of their task for the acquisition of noble virtues.

48. O purified through knowledge and righteousness, O patient teacher of

grammar, just as I a seeker after knowledge, and a firm gleaner of wisdom, wash out the sin that I have committed through my senses and the mortal body, so do thou O God, preserve me from tortuous sin.

49. The oblation full of cooked articles put into the fire, goes up to the sky. and returns therefrom full of rain.

O God, Let us twain, like traders, barter our food and strength.

50. Give me this article and I will give you that in return. Keep this as my deposit, I keep this as your deposit. Give me the cash price for it. I give you the price demanded. Let people thus transact business truthfully.

51. Thou chairman, just as comrades, luminous in themselves, pleasing others, advanced in knowledge, with their sharpest intellect, do verily praise God, and being regaled with nutritious diet, overcome miseries, so do thou yoke thy vigour and prowess with them.

52. We revere Thee, O God of Bounty, Who art fair to see. Being praised by us, O best companion, Thou fulfillest all our desires. O Lord, yoke Thy vigour and prowess for us.

53. By reflecting on the merits of the learned, and following the

54. May we get in future births again and again the mind, for doing virtuous deeds, for acquiring strength, for longevity, and contem- plation of God'for long.

55. O venerable elders, may this man endowed with godly qualities, give us in this and the next life, intellect whereby we may enjoy a long life and perform noble deeds.

56. O God, acting upon Thy Law, possessing mental self-conscious- ness in healthy bodies, blest with progeny, let us enjoy happiness.

57. O learned person, the chastiser of the sinful and the unright- eous, all these eatable things are for thee. Accept them with thy know- ledge and vedic lore. O learned man, follow the Veda and the law of Dharma. O learned person, accept the food worth eating which uproots all diseases.

58. May we ward off all calamities by worshipping God, Who is unchangeable in the past, presenr and future, chastises the sinners, and is highly benevolent. Just as God makes us better housed, more prosperous, and determined so may we adore Him.

59. O God, Thou art the healer of the physical, mental and spiri- tual maladies. Heal, Thou the sufferings of cow, horse and all mankind. Grant happiness to ram and ewe.

60. We worship the Omnipresent, Pure God, Who augments our

61. O hero, the chastiser of enemies, and expert in the art of war, with bow extended, with self-protecting trident, with full armour, with grace and power, meet thy foes on the other side of the mountain. With thy this power of protection, come to us, without causing us any harm. 62. May we be endowed with triple life, as a truth-seer sage, or the custodian of knowledge through the grace of God, is endowed with, or as the learned persons enjoy triple life.

63. O God, Thou art certainly the Embodiment* of grace, self- Existent, our Father, obeisance be to Thee. Harm me not. I approach Thee for long life, for nice food, for progeny, for riches in abundance, for noble children, and for heroic vigour.

CHAPTER IV

1. May we, on this earth, where reside happily all the learned persons, be able to revere the sages

May we acting on the teachings of the Rig, Sam and Yajur Vedas, end all our miseries. May we rejoice in food and growth of riches. These pure, disease-killing waters be gracious to me. May the herbs protect me Thou armed king, harm not the worshipper.

2. May waters, like mother, purify our bodies. May the waters purified by clarified butter, purify us through rain. Pure waters remove all our physical imperfections.

May I advance in life, being bright and pure through waters. Through celibacy and abstemiousness may I possess a body, healthy, comfortable, excellent, beautiful and strong.

3. O Sun, thou bringest rain on different parts of the earth. Giver of splendour art thou bestow on me the gift of splendour. The disperser of cloud art thou with thy brilliance. The giver of eye art thou. Give we the gift of vision.

4. Purify me, the Lord of Purity. Purify me, the Lord of knowledge, Purify me, the Lord of the Vedas.

O Lord, Creator of the universe, purify me, through sun-beams and thy immortal purifying knowledge.

O Master of the purified souls, may I full of lofty sentiments accom- plish the desire actuated by which, through your grace, I purify myself.

5. O sages, we admire your praiseworthy qualities, during the performance of this happy sacrifice. O sages, we beg of you the fulfilment of our desires pertaining to the sacrifice.

6. O men, just as I actively and wisely commence performing the sacrifice, with vedic texts, with cultured tongue, with wisdom- teaching voice, with a tongue full of sweetness and truth, in an orderly and well-directed way, with the help of the extended firmament, Earth, sky and air, so do Ye.

7. We perform the yajna for resolution for good religious acts, for kindling fire, for the propagation of the Vedas, for the development of wisdom, for the enhancement of knowledge, for utilizing lightning, for philanthropy, for following the laws of Dharma, for austerity, for digestive faculty, for learning and teaching, for eloquent and weighty speech, for worshipping rightly God, for purifying gastric juice, and for practising Truth.

Ye, meritorious, all-beneficial divine waters, Ye Heaven and Earth and spacious air between them, we serve with Oblation.

8. May every mortal man seek the friendship of the Guiding God. May we all have recourse to the use of arms for the acquisition of due wealth. May every man acquire riches and become strong through wise deeds.

9. After the study of the Rig and Yajur Vedas, I commence using their scientific aspLCts, i.e., theoretical and practical. They protect m? in this yajna, in which vedic texts are recited. O yajna, thou art happiness, give me happiness ; here are these oblations of corn for thee ; forbear to harm me.

10. O learned person, may mechanical science, perfected by the application of fire, the giver of light, bestow strength on me. It is the guardian of manifold objects, giver of happiness to the learned, the mechanic, and the source of prosperity, make the crops produce abundant grain through its aid. O learned person, depend on thyself for advancement. Protect me from the misery of sin. Accomplish this yajna with the recitation of vedic texts.

11. Take a vow. God is Agni. Yajna is Agni. God, the Guardian of our soul, is fit for worship. For the attainment of an ideal, I long for divine, pleasant, radiant intelligence that unites me with God. May that intelligence, that makes me happily cross the ocean of this mundane existence, be within my control.

May the philosophic, meditative and energetic sages urge us on to noble deeds, may they be our protectors. We invoke them from the inmost recesses of our heart.

12. O men, the waters that we have ,lrunk, staying within our belly, give us peace, riches, freedom from consumption, disease, and pangs of hunger and thirst. They are the strengthened of our true knowledge, full of divine qualities, and undying flavours. May they be pleasant to your taste.

13. O learned man, just as this sacrificial body of thine, protects the vital breaths and the people, and thou forsakest it not, so do I not forsake it without enjoying the full span of life. Just as disease curing and pure waters flow on the earth, so shouldst thou live in the world wisely ; and so do I.

14. The fire, which keeps us active in our wakeful state, makes us take joy in most refreshing sleep. It protects us free from idleness and casts away the idlers. We should use this fire properly which deals with us again and again.

15. I get back after rebirth mind, life, bre.ith, soul, eyes and ears. May God the Leader of all, Non-violent, Omniscient, Guardian of our souls, save us from misfortune and sin.

16. O God, Thou art the Guardian of sacred vows among mankind. Thou art meet for praise at holy rites. O Giver of Splendour, Come unto us, grant us wealth, give us more. God, the Creator, the Giver of wealth, gives us riches.

17. O learned person, this body thou hast got and reared is for the meditation of God and sacrifice. Through this body, being vigorous, gain splendour and lustre. Be active through knowledge.

18. O resplendent God, in this world created by Thee, may I obtain mastery over the vast power of speech. O Speech, thou art pure, pleasant and dear to the sages.

19. O Speech, thou art thought, mind, intelligence, giver of knowledge and victory ; thou art power, worthy of worship, immortal, and double-headed. May thou give us comfort in the past and future. May breathe, the strength giving friend of time advance thee in knowledge, and guard thy pathways for God, whose eye is over all.

20. O man, may thy mother, thy father, thy own brother, and thy friend of the same society grant thee leave to tread on the path ordained by God.

O speech, for the acquisition of splendour, may thou unite with God, the Prompter of all. May the Celibate student choose thee.

May thou, O man, happily acquire again and again this speech, the friend of the learned.

21. O speech, thou art all-pervading, eternal, lustrous, sublime and pleasant. The learned person uses thee for happiness. The sage, the chastiser of the wicked longs for thee along with other educated persons.

22. O speech, I use thee in the heights of sky and the sacri- ficial places on the Earth. Thou art the preserver of vedic verses. May thou be enriched with high knowledge. May thou rest in us. May thou be united to us. Thou art rich. May I be full of riches. Let us not be deprived of abundant riches. May splendour reside in thee full of understanding.

23. O speech, I praise thee with divine, ignorance-removing and penetrating intelligence. End not my life. I will not through ignorance spoil thee. O vedic text, in thy protection, may I be blessed with heroism.

24. O learned person "This is thy share of the sacrifice allied with Gayatri verses" so may he say unto me a student of science. This is thy share of the sacrifice allied with Trishtup verses/ so may he say unto me, the seeker of the essence of things. This is thy share of the sacrifice allied with verses in Jagati metre/ so may he say unto me a student of science. 'May thou attain to sovereignty detailed in vedic-verses in all other metres/ May he thus preach the art of kingship unto me, full of affluence, O learned persons, just as ye are our purifying preachers, so am I your worthy disciple, endowed with virtues and wealth. May ye develop me and this sacrifice (yajna) as well.

25. I adore God, the Creator of the Earth and Sky, the Source of all Knowledge, the Embodiment of Splendour, the Sustainer of all the beautiful planets, the Centre of love, the object of praise by the Vedas, and their Revealer. His lofty effulgent Self is divulged in the created world. He has fixed the bright sun and the

moon in their conduct. He is the wisest Actor. His mercy grants us happiness. O God I worship Thee as Bestower of happiness on mankind. May all mortals enjoy life, through Thee. May Thou grant life to all human beings.

26. In the yajna, we should please the learned performer by offering him cash and kind. May the praiseworthy brilliance of the sun make me strong through its thousandfold abundance. O wise person, may we also obtain the riches, which thou hast secured through thy rule over the earth. Just as I accomplish the sacrifice through noble, pure sentiments, earn gold with gold, attain to salvation through immortal knowledge, so may thou.

27. O king, famous for eloquence, brilliance, enmity to fraud, antagonism to the thoughtless, pleasing manners, dexterity, defeating the designs of the ill-minded, friendship, and the art of befriending others, with longing for delight, come into us.

May thou, with a beautiful and healthy body, and endowed with all cherished objects, enjoy enviable happiness. These intelligent and faith- full subjects and servants, who all round protect you, should be protected by you to ward off your enemy from doing injury unto you.

28. Oh God, dissuade me from sin, and establish me firmly in righteousness. May I enjoy the pleasures of final beatitude by leading a long and virtuous life.

29. May we tread the path free from sin, and full of delight, by which a wise man overcomes all carnal pleasures, and gathers wealth.

30. O God, Thou art the protector of the Earth, O Mighty Lord, Thou fixed the Earth in its Orbit. Thou Controllest the Sun. Thou hast created the beautiful sky. O Lord of all, thou fixest in space all the worlds. All these are the works of Him alone, so do we know.

31. We should worship God, who hast created the sky over the forests, put speed in horses, milk in cows, intellect in hearts, gastric juice in men, sun in heaven, and medicinal plants like Soma in the mountains.

32. O God, where resplendent through Thy qualities of knowledge, Thou art known by the learned, and where Thou Greatest lustrous eyes, the instruments for seeing the sun and fire, there we worship Thee.

33. Let man and woman, who study the vedas kill not their heroes, are limited in resources, be ever joyous, who live together and are fit to bear the burden of domestic life, be united together in married life. May such couples visit the houses of religious persons and give them happiness.

34. O learned man, the Lord of Earth, thou art my gracious helper. Fly happily to all the stations in our well overhauled aeroplane. Doing so, let not thieves, robbers, and malignant opponents meet thee. Fall like a falcon upon such foes. Go to the houses of religious persons, situated in distant parts of the world.

35. Do homage unto God, the Friend of all, Ever Pure, and Res- plendent. Worship the true nature of the Mighty God. Sing praises unto God, the Purifier of all radiant objects, the Omniscient, the Embodi- ment of virtues, and the Exhibitor of distant objects.

36. O God, Thou art the Director of this fine world ; the Creator of objects dependable on air, and the Force inherent in the sun for the motion of waters, the stay and support of all excellent objects. O Lord, Thou makest us reach the destination of true and high knowledge.

37. O God, just as learned persons, utilize Thy created objects by Oblations, so should we utilize all of them. Thy Yajna is the advancer of our progeny, wealth and houses, dispeller of diseases, bestower of heroes, remover of the idlers and cowards from amongst us, and giver of happiness in manifold ways, may that conduce to our benefit. O learned persons, may ye perform this yajna, and live happily in your houses.

Atharva Veda

BOOK 1

HYMN I

A prayer to Vāchaspati for divine illumination and help.

1 Now may Vāchaspati assign to me the strength and powers of those

Who, wearing every shape and form, the triple seven, are wandering round.

2 Come thou again, Vāchaspati, come with divine intelligence.

Vasoshpati, repose thou here. In me be Knowledge, yea, in me.

3 Here, even here, spread sheltering arms like the two bow-ends strained with cord.

This let Vāchaspati confirm. In me be Knowledge, yea, in me.

4 Vāchaspati hath been invoked: may he invite us in reply.

May we adhere to Sacred Lore. Never may I be reft thereof.

HYMN II

A charm against dysentery

1 We know the father of the shaft, Parjanya, liberal nourisher,

Know well his mother: Prithivī, Earth with her manifold designs.

2 Do thou, O Bowstring, bend thyself around us: make my body stone.

Firm in thy strength drive far away malignities and hateful things.

3 When, closely clinging round the wood, the bowstring sings triumph to the swift and whizzing arrow,

Indra, ward off from us the shaft, the missile.

4 As in its flight the arrow's point hangs between earth and firmament,

So stand this Munja grass between ailment and dysenteric ill!

HYMN III

A charm against constipation and suppression of urine

1 We know the father of the shaft, Parjanya strong with hundred powers:

By this may I bring health unto thy body: let the channels pour their burthen freely as of old.

2 We know the father of the shaft, Mitra, the Lord of hundred powers:

By this, etc.

3 We know the father of the shaft, Varuna, strong with hundred powers:

By this, etc.

4 We know the father of the shaft, the Moon endowed with hundred powers:

By this, etc.

5 We know the father of the shaft, the Sun endowed with hundred powers:

By this may I bring health unto thy body: let the channels pour their burthen freely as of old.

6 Whate'er hath gathered, as it flowed, in bowels, bladder, or in groins,

Thus let the conduit, free from check, pour all its burthen as of old.

7 I lay the passage open as one cleaves the dam that bars the lake:

Thus let, etc.

8 Now hath the portal been unclosed as, of the sea that holds the flood:

Thus let, etc.

9 Even as the arrow flies away when loosened from the archer's bow,

Thus let the burthen be discharged from channels that are checked no more.

HYMN IV

To the waters, for the prosperity of cattle

1 Along their paths the Mothers go, sisters of priestly ministrants,

Blending their water with the mead.

2 May yonder Waters near the Sun, or those wherewith the Sun is joined,

Send forth this sacrifice of ours.

3 I call the Waters, Goddesses, hitherward where our cattle drink:

The streams must share the sacrifice.

4 Amrit is in the Waters, in the Waters balm.

Yea, through our praises of the Floods, O horses, be ye fleet and strong, and, O ye kine, be full of strength.

HYMN V

To the waters, for strength and power

1 Ye, Waters, truly bring us bliss: so help us to strength and power

That we may look on great delight.

2 Here grant to us a share of dew, that most auspicious dew of yours,

Like mothers in their longing love.

3 For you we fain would go to him to whose abode ye send us forth,

And, Waters, give us procreant strength.

4 I pray the Floods to send us balm, those who bear rule o'er precious things,

And have supreme control of men.

HYMN VI

To the waters, for health and wealth

1 The Waters be to us for drink, Goddesses, for our aid and bliss:

Let them stream health and wealth to us.

2 Within the Waters—Soma thus hath told me—dwell all balms that heal,

And Agni, he who blesseth all.

3 O Waters, teem with medicine to keep my body safe from harm,

So that I long may see the Sun.

4 The Waters bless us, all that rise in desert lands or marshy pools!

Bless us the Waters dug from earth, bless us the Waters brought

in jars, bless us the Waters of the Rains!

HYMN VII

To Indra and Agni, for the detection and destruction of evil spirits

1 Bring the Kimidin hither, bring the Yātudhāna self-declared

For Agni, God, thou, lauded, hast become the Dasyu's slaughterer.

2 O Jātavedas, Lord Supreme, controller of our bodies, taste

The butter, Agni, taste the oil: make thou the Yātudhānas mourn.

3 Let Yātudhānas mourn, let all greedy Kimidins weep and wail:

And, Agni, Indra, may ye both accept this sacrifice of ours.

4 May Agni seize upon them first, may strong-armed Indra drive them forth:

Let every wicked sorcerer come hither and say, Here am I.

5 Let us behold thy strength, O Jātavedas. Viewer of men, tell us the Yātudhānas.

Burnt by thy heat and making declaration let all approach this sacrifice before thee.

6 O Jātavedas, seize, on them: for our advantage art thou born:

Agni, be thou our messenger and make the Yātudhānas wail.

7 O Agni, bring thou hitherward the Yātudhānas bound and chained.

And afterward let Indra tear their heads off with his thunderbolt.

HYMN VIII

To Indra, Brihaspati, Soma and Agni, for the destruction of sorcerers

1 This sacrifice shall bring the Yātudhānas as the flood brings foam:

Here let the doer of this deed woman or man, acknowledge it.

2 This one hath come confessing all: do ye receive him eagerly.

Master him thou, Brihaspati; Agni and Soma, pierce him through.

3 O Soma-drinker, strike and bring the Yātudhāna's progeny:

Make the confessing sinner's eyes fall from his head, both right and left.

4 As thou, O Agni Jātavedas, knowest the races of these secret greedy beings,

So strengthened by the power of prayer, O Agni, crushing them down a hundred times destroy them.

HYMN IX

Benediction on a King at his inauguration

1 May Indra, Pūshan, Varuria, Mitra, Agni, benignant Gods, maintain this man in riches.

May the Ādityas and the Vive Devas set and support him in supremest lustre.

2 May light, O Gods, be under his dominion, Agni, the Sun, all; that is bright and golden.

Prostrate beneath our feet his foes and rivals. Uplift him to the loftiest cope of heaven.

3 Through that most mighty prayer, O Jātavedas, wherewith thou brought milk to strengthen Indra,

Even therewith exalt this man, O Agni, and give him highest rank among his kinsmen.

4 I have assumed their sacrifice, O Agni, their hopes, their glory, and their riches' fullness.

Prostrate beneath our feet his foes and rivals. Uplift him to the loftiest cope of heaven.

HYMN X

Absolution of a sinner after intercession with Varuna

1 This Lord is the Gods' ruler; for the wishes of Varuna the King must be accomplished.

Therefore, triumphant with the prayer I utter, I rescue this man from the Fierce One's anger.

2 Homage be paid, King Varuna, to thine anger; for thou, dread God, detectest every falsehood.

I send a thousand others forth together: let this thy servant live a hundred autumns.

3 Whatever falsehood thou hast told, much evil spoken with the tongue,

I liberate thee from the noose of Varuna the righteous King.

4 I free thee from Vaisvānara, from the great surging flood of sin.

Call thou thy brothers, Awful One! And pay attention to our prayer.

HYMN XI

A charm to be used at child-birth

1 Vashat to thee. O Pūshan At this birth let Aryaman the Sage perform as Hotar-priest,

As one who bears in season let this dame be ready to bring forth her child.

2 Four are the regions of the sky, and four the regions of the earth:

The Gods have brought the babe; let them prepare the woman for the birth.

3 Puerpera (infatem) detegat: nos uterum aperimus. Lexa teipsam,

puerpera. Tu, parturiens! emitte eum non carni, ncn adipi, non medullae adhāerntem.

4 Descendat viscosa placenta, cani, comedenda placenta; decidat placenta.

5 Diffindo tuum urinae ductum, diffindo vaginam, diffindo inguina.

Matrem natumque divido, puerum a placenta divido: decidat placenta.

6 Sicut ventus, sicut mens, sicut alites volant, sic, decem mensium

puer, cum placenta descende: descendat placenta.

Book 2

HYMN I

Glorification of the prime cause of all things

1 Vena beholds That Highest which lies hidden, wherein this all resumes one form and fashion.

Thence Prisni milked all life that had existence: the hosts that know the light with songs extolled her.

2 Knowing Eternity, may the Gandharva declare to us that highest secret station.

Three steps thereof lie hidden in the darkness: he who knows these shall be the father's father.

3 He is our kinsman, father, and begetter: he knows all beings and all Ordinances.

He only gave the Gods their appellations: all creatures go to him to ask direction.

4 I have gone forth around the earth and heaven, I have approached the first-born Son of Order.

He, putting voice, as 'twere, within the speaker, stands in the world, he, verily is Agni.

5 I round the circumjacent worlds have travelled to see the far extended thread of Order.

Wherein the Gods, obtaining life eternal, have risen upward to one common birthplace.

HYMN II

A charm to ensure success in gambling

1 Lord of the World, divine Gandharva, only he should be honoured in the Tribes and worshipped.

Fast with my spell, celestial God, I hold thee. Homage to thee! Thy home is in the heavens.

2 Sky-reaching, like the Sun in brightness, holy, he who averts from us the Gods' displeasure.

Lord of the World, may the Gandharva bless us, the friendly God who only must be worshipped.

3 I came, I met these faultless, blameless beings: among the Apsarases was the Gandharva.

Their home is in the sea—so men have told me,—whence they come quickly hitherward and vanish.

4 Thou, Cloudy! ye who follow the Gandharva Visvā-vasu, ye,

Starry! Lightning-Flasher!

You, O ye Goddesses, I truly worship.

5 Haunters of darkness, shrill in voice, dice-lovers, maddeners of the mind

To these have I paid homage, the Gandharva's wives, Apsarases.

HYMN III

A water-cure charm

1 That little spring of water which is running downward from the hill

I turn to healing balm for thee that thou mayst be good medicine.

2 Hither and onward! Well! Come on! Among thy hundred remedies

Most excellent of all art thou, curing disease and morbid flow.

3 The Asuras bury deep in earth this mighty thing that healeth wounds.

This is the cure for morbid flow, this driveth malady away.

4 The emmets from the water-flood produce this healing medicine:

This is the cure for morbid flow, this driveth malady away.

5 Mighty is this wound-healing balm: from out the earth was it produced.

This is the cure for morbid flow, this driveth malady away.

6 Bless us the Waters! be the Plants auspicious!

May Indra's thunderbolt drive off the demons. Far from us fall the shafts they shoot against us!

HYMN IV

A charm to ensure health and prosperity by wearing an amulet

1 For length of life, for mighty joy, uninjured, ever showing strength.

We wear Vishkandha's antidote, the Amulet of Jangida.

2 Amulet of a thousand powers, Jangida save us, all around.

From Jambha, and from Viara, Vishkandha, and tormenting pain.

3 This overcomes Vishkandha, this chases the greedy fiends away:

May this our panacea, may Jangida save us from distress.

4 With Jangida that brings delight, Amulet given by the Gods.

We in the conflict overcome Vishkandha and all Rākshasas.

5 May Cannabis and Jangida preserve me from Vishkandha — that

Brought to us from the forest, this sprung from the saps of husbandry.

6 This Amulet destroys the might of magic and malignity:

So may victorious Jangida prolong the years we have to live.

HYMN V

Invitation to, and praise of Indra

1 Indra, be gracious, drive thou forth, come, Hero, with thy two bay steeds.

Taste the libation, hither, enjoying meath and the hymn, come, fair, to the banquet.

2 O Indra, even as one athirst, fill thee with meath as 'twere from heaven.

Sweet-toned, the raptures of this juice have come to thee as to the light.

3 Swift-conquering Indra, Mitra like, smote, as a Yati, Vritra dead.

Like Bhrigu he cleft Vala through, and quelled his foes in Soma's rapturous joy.

4 O Indra, let the juices enter thee. Fill full thy belly, sate thee, mighty one! Let the hymn bring thee.

Hear thou my call, accept the song I sing, here, Indra, with thy friends enjoy thyself, to height of rapture.

5 Now will I tell the manly deeds of Indra, the first that he achieved, the thunder-wielder.

He slew the Dragon, then disclosed the waters, and cleft the channels of the mountain torrents.

6 He slew the Dragon lying on the mountain: his heavenly bolt of thunder Tvashtar fashioned.

Like lowing kine in rapid flow descending the waters glided downward to the ocean.

7 Impetuous as a bull he chose the Soma, and quaffed the juices in three sacred beakers.

Maghavan grasped the thunder for his weapon, and smote to death this first-born of the dragons.

BOOK 3

HYMN I

A prayer or charm for the defeat and destruction of enemies in battle

1 Let the wise Agni go against our foemen, burning against ill-will and imprecation

Let him bewilder our opponents' army, Let Jātavedas smite and make them handless.

2 Mighty are ye for such a deed, O Maruts. Go forward, overcome them and destroy them.

The Vasus slew, and these were left imploring. Wise Agni as our messenger assail them!

3 O Maghavan, O Indra, thou who slayest fiends, and, Agni, thou,

Burn, both of you, against these men, the foeman's host that threatens us.

4 Shot down the slope, with thy two tawny coursers, forth go thy bolt, destroying foes, O Indra!

Slay those who fly, slay those who stand and follow.

On every side fulfil these men's intention.

5 Indra, bewilder thou the foemen's army.

With Agni's, Vāta's furious rush drive them away to every side.

6 Let Indra daze their army. Let the Maruts slay it with their might.

Let Agni take their eyes away, and let the conquered host retreat.

HYMN II

A rifaccimento or recension of I

1 May Agni, he who knows, our envoy, meet them, burning against ill-will and imprecation.

May he bewilder our opponent's senses. May Jātavedas smite and make them handless.

2 This Agni hath bewildered all the senses that were in your hearts:

Now let him blast you from your home, blast you away from every side.

3 Dazing their senses, Indra, come hitherward with the wish and will.

With Agni's, Vāta's furious rush drive them to every side away.

4 Vanish, ye hopes and plans of theirs, be ye confounded, all their thoughts!

Whatever wish is in their heart, do thou expel it utterly.

5 Bewildering the senses of our foemen, seize on their bodies and depart, O Apvā!

Go meet them, flame within their hearts and burn them. Smite thou the foes with darkness and amazement.

6 That army of our enemies, O Maruts, that comes against us with its might, contending—

Meet ye and strike it with unwelcome darkness so that not one of them may know another.

HYMN III

A charm for the restoration of an expelled king

1 Loudly he roared. Here let him labour deftly. Spread, Agni, over spacious earth and heaven.

Let Maruts who possesses all treasures yoke thee. Bring him who reverently paid oblations.

2 Though he be far away, let the red horses bring Indra, bring the sage to us and friendship,

Since with Sautrāmani Gods for him o'erpower Gāyatri, Brihatī, and hymn of praises.

3 King Varuna call thee hither from the waters! From hills and mountains Soma call thee hither!

Let Indra call thee hither to these people. Fly hither to these people as a falcon.

4 May the hawk bring the man who must be summoned, from far away, in alien land, an exile.

May both the Asvins make thy pathway easy. Come, and unite yourselves with him, ye Kinsmen.

5 Let thine opponents call thee back. Thy friends have chosen, thee again.

Indra and Agni, all the Gods have kept thy home amid the tribe.

6 He who disputes our calling thee, be he a stranger or akin.

Drive him, O Indra, far away, and do thou bring this man to us.

HYMN IV

A benediction at the election of a king

1 To thee hath come the kingship with its splendour: On! Shine as lord, sole ruler of the people.

King! let all regions of the heavens invite thee. Here let men wait on thee and bow before thee.

2 The tribesmen shall elect thee for the Kingship, these five celestial regions shall elect thee.

Rest on the height and top of kingly power: thence as a mighty man award us treasures.

3 Kinsmen, inviting thee, shall go to meet thee, with thee go Agni as an active herald.

Let women and their sons be friendly-minded. Thou mighty one, shalt see abundant tribute.

4 First shall the Asvins, Varuna and Mitra, the Universal Gods, and Maruts call thee.

Then turn thy mind to giving gifts of treasures, thence, mighty one, distribute wealth among us.

5 Speed to us hither from the farthest distance. Propitious unto thee be Earth and Heaven.

Even so hath Varuna this King asserted, he who himself hath called thee: come thou hither.

6 Pass to the tribes of men. O Indra, Indra. Thou the Varunas hast been found accordant.

To his own place this one hath called thee, saying, Let him adore the Gods and guide the clansmen.

7 The Bounteous Paths in sundry forms and places, all in accord, have given thee room and comfort.

Let all of these in concert call thee hither. Live thy tenth decade here, a strong kind ruler.

HYMN V

A King's address to an amulet which is to strengthen his authority

1 This Parna-Amulet hath come, strong and destroying with its strength my rivals.

The power of the Gods, the plants' sweet essence, may it incite me ceaselessly with vigour.

2 O Parna-Amulet, in me set firmly might and opulence.

Within the compass of my rule may I be rooted and supreme.

3 That dear mysterious Amulet which Gods have set within the tree,

May the Gods grant to me to wear together with extended life.

4 As Indra's gift, by Varuna instructed, Parna hath come, the mighty strength of Soma:

This would I, brightly shining, love and cherish for long life lasting through a hundred autumns.

5 The Parna-Charm hath come to me for great security from ill.

That I may be exalted, yea, above the wealth of Aryaman.

6 Sagacious builders of the car, cleaver and skilful artisans,—

Make all the men on every side, Parna, obedient to my will

7 The kings and makers of the kings, troop-leaders, masters of the horse,

Make all the men on every side, Parna, obedient to my will.

8 Thou, Parna, art my body's guard, man kin my birth to me a man.

With splendour of the circling year I bind thee on me, Amulet!

HYMN VI

Address to an amulet which is to secure the defeat of the wearer's enemies

1 Masculine springs from masculine, Asvattha grows from Khadira,

May it destroy mine enemies, who hate me and whom I detest.

2 Crush down my foes, Asvattha! Rend, O Burster, those who storm and rage,

With Indra, slayer of the fiends, with Mitra and with Varuna.

3 As thou hast rent and torn apart, Asvattha! in the mighty sea,

So rend asundar all those men who hate me and whom I detest.

4 Thou who like some victorious bull displayest thy surpassing might.

With thee, with thee, Asvattha! We would overcome our enemies.

5 Nirriti bind them with the bonds of Death which never may be loosed.

Mine enemies, Asvattha! Those who hate me and whom I detest.

6 As thou, Asvastha!, mountest on the trees and overthrowest them,

So do thou break my foeman's head asunder and o'erpower him.

7 Let them drift downward like a boat torn from the rope that fastened it.

There is no turning back for those whom He who Cleaves hath driven away.

8 With mental power I drive them forth, drive them with intellect and charm.

We banish and expel them with the branch of an Asvattha tree.

HYMN VII

A charm with an amulet of buck horn to drive away hereditary disease

1 The fleet-foot Roebuck wears upon his head a healing remedy.

Innate disease he drives away to all directions with his horn.

2 With his four feet the vigorous Buck hath bounded in pursuit of thee.

Unbind the chronic sickness, Horn! Deeply inwoven in the heart.

3 That which shines younder, like a roof resting on four walls, down on us,—

Therewith from out thy body we drive all the chronic malady,

4 May those twin stars, auspicious, named Releasers, up in yonder sky.

Loose of the chronic malady the uppermost and lowest bond.

5 Water, indeed, hath power to heal, Water drives malady away.

May water—for it healeth all—free thee from permanent disease.

6 Hath some prepared decoction brought inveterate disease on thee,

I know the balm that healeth it: we drive the malady away.

7 What time the starlight disappears, what time the gleams of dawn depart,

May evil fortune pass from us, the chronic sickness disappear.

HYMN VIII

A charm to secure the submission, love, and fidelity of kinsmen

1 Let Mitra come, arranging, with the Seasons, lulling the Earth to rest with gleams of splendour.

And so let Agni, Varuna, and Vāyu make our dominion tranquil and exalted.

2 May Indra, Tvashtar hear my word with favour, may Dhātar, Rāti, Savitar accept it.

I call the Goddess Aditi, heroes' mother, that I may be the centre of my kinsmen.

3 Soma I call, and Savitar with homage, and all the Ādityas in the time of contest.

Long may this fire send forth its splendour, lighted by kinsmen uttering no word against me.

4 Here, verily, may you stay: go ye no farther. The strong Herd,

Lord of Increase, drive you hither!

To please this man may all the Gods together come unto you and be as dames who love him.

5 We bend together all your minds, your vows and purposes we bend.

We bend together you who stand apart with hopes opposed to ours.

6 I with my spirit seize and hold your spirits. Follow with thought and wish my thoughts and wishes.

I make your hearts the thralls of my dominion; on me attendant come thy way I guide you.

HYMN IX

A charm against rheumatism (vishkondha)

1 Heaven is the sire, the mother Earth, of Karsapha and Visapha.

As ye have brought them hither, Gods! So do ye move them hence away.

2 The bands hold fast without a knot: this is the way that Manu used.

I make Vishkandha impotent as one emasculateth bulls.

3 Then to a tawny-coloured string the wise and skilful bind a brush.

Let bandages make impotent the strong and active Kābava.

4 Ye who move active in your strength like Gods with Asuras' magic powers,

Even as the monkey scorns the dogs, Bandages! Scorn the Kābava.

5 Yea, I will chide thee to thy shame, I will disgrace the Kābava.

Under our impracations ye, like rapid cars, shall pass away.

6 One and one hundred over earth are the Vishkandhas spread abroad.

Before these have they fetched thee forth. Vishkandha quelling Amulet.

HYMN X

A new year prayer

1 The First hath dawned. With Yama may it be a cow to pour forth milk.

May she be rich in milk and stream for us through many a coming year.

2 May she whom Gods accept with joy, Night who approacheth as a cow,

She who is Consort of the Year, bring us abundant happiness

3 Thou whom with reverence we approach, O Night, as model of the Year,

Us children long to live; bless us with increase of our wealth.

4 This same is she whose light first dawned upon us: she moves established in the midst of others:

Great powers and glories are contained within her: a first-born bride, she conquers and bears children.

5 Loud was the wooden pass-gear's ring and rattle, as it made annual oblation ready.

First Ashtakā! May we be lords of riches, with goodly children and good men about us.

6 The shrine of Ilā flows with oil and fatness: accept, O Jātavedas, our oblations.

Tame animals of varied form and colour—may all the seven abide with me contented.

7 Come thou to nourish me and make me prosper. Night! May the favour of the Gods attend us.

Filled full, O Ladle, fly thou forth. Completely filled fly back again.

Serving at every sacrifice bring to us food and energy.

8 This Year hath come to us, thy lord and consort, O Ekāshtakā.

Vouchsafe us children long to live, bless us with increase of our wealth.

9 The Seasons, and the Seasons' Lords I worship, annual parts and groups.

Half years, Years, Months, I offer to the Lord of all existing things.

10 I offer to the Seasons, to their several groups, to Months, to Years.

Dhātar, Vidhātar, Fortune, to the lord of all existing things.

11 With fatness and libation we sacrifice and adore the Gods.

Wealthy in kine may we retire to rest us in our modest homes.

12 Ekāshtakā, burning with zealous fervour, brought forth her babe the great and glorious Indra.

With him the Gods subdued their adversaries: the Lord of Might became the Dasyus' slayer.

13 Indra's and Soma's mother! Thou art daughter of Prajāpati.

Satisfy thou our hearts' desires. Gladly accept our sacrifice.

HYMN XI

A charm for the recovery of a dangerously sick man

1 For life I set thee free by this oblation both from unmarked'.

Decline and from consumption:

Or if the grasping demon have possessed him, free him from her,

O Indra, thou and Agni!

2 Be his days ended, be he now departed, be he brought very near to death already,

Out of Destruction's lap again I bring him, save him for life to last a hundred autumns.

3 With sacrifice thousand-eyed and hundred-powered, bringing a hundred lives, have I restored him,

That Indra through the autumns may conduct him safe to the farther shore of all misfortune.

4 Live, waxing in thy strength a hundred autumns, live through a hundred springs, a hundred winters!

Indra, Agni, Savitar, Brihaspati give thee a hundred! With hundred-lived oblation have I saved him,

5 Breath, Respiration, come to him, as two car-oxen to their stall!

Let all the other deaths, whereof men count a hundred, pass away.

6 Breath, Respiration, stay ye here. Go ye not hence away from him,

Bring, so that he may reach old age, body and members back again.

7 I give thee over to old age, make thee the subject of old age.

Let kindly old age lead thee on. Let all the other deaths, whereof men count a hundred, pass away!

8 Old age hath girt thee with its bonds even as they bind a bull with rope.

The death held thee at thy birth bound with a firmly-knotted noose,

Therefrom, with both the hands of Truth, Brihaspati hath loosened thee.

HYMN XII

A benediction on a newly built house

1 Here, even here I fix my firm-set dwelling; flowing with fatness may it stand in safety.

May we approach thee, House! With all our people, uncharmed and goodly men, and dwell within thee,

2 Even here, O House, stand thou on firm foundation, wealthy in horses, rich in kine and gladness.

Wealthy in nourishment. in milk and fatness, rise up for great felicity and fortune.

3 A spacious store, O House, art thou, full of clean corn and lofty-roofed.

Let the young calf and little boy approach thee, and milch-kine streaming homeward in the evening.

4 This House may Savitar and Vāyu stablish, Brihaspati who knows the way, and Indra.

May the moist Maruts sprinkle it with fatness, and may King Bhaga make our corn-land fruitful.

5 Queen of the home! thou, sheltering, kindly Goddess, was established by the Gods in the beginning.

Clad in thy robe of grass be friendly-minded, and give us wealth with goodly men about us.

6 Thou Pole, in ordered fashion mount the pillar. Strong, shining forth afar, keep off our foemen.

House! let not those who dwell within thee suffer. Live we with all our men, a hundred autumns.

7 To this the tender boy hath come, to this the calf with all the beasts,

To this crock of foaming drink, hither with jars of curdled milk.

8 Bring hitherward, O dame, the well-filled pitcher, the stream of molten butter blent with nectar.

Bedew these drinkers with a draught of Amrit.

May all our hopes' fulfilment guard this dwelling.

9 Water that kills Consumption, free from all Consumption, here I bring.

With Agni, the immortal one, I enter and possess the house.

HYMN XIII

A benediction on a newly cut water channel

1 As ye, when Ahi had been slain, flowed forth together with a roar,

So are ye called the Roaring Ones: this, O ye Rivers, is your name.

2 As driven forth by Varuna ye swiftly urged your rolling waves,

There Indra reached you as you flowed; hence ye are still the water-floods.

3 Indra restrained you with his might. Goddesses, as ye glided on

Not in accordance with his will: hence have ye got the name of streams.

4 One only God set foot on you flowing according to your will,

The mighty ones breathed upward fast: hence; Water is the name they bear.

5 Water is good, water indeed is fatness. Agni and Soma, truly, both bring water.

May the strong rain of those who scatter sweetness come helpful unto me with breath and vigour.

6 Then verily, I see, yea, also hear them: their sound approaches me, their voice comes hither.

Even then I think I am enjoying Amrit, what time I drink my fill of you, gold coloured!

7 Here, O ye Waters, is your heart. Here is your calf, ye holy ones.

Flow here, just here, O mighty Streams, whither I now am leading you.

HYMN XIV

A benediction on a cattle pen

1 A Pen wherein to dwell at ease, abundance and prosperity,

Whate'er is called the birth of day, all this do we bestow on you.

2 May Aryaman pour gifts on you, and Pūshan, land Brihaspati,

And Indra, winner of the prize. Make ye my riches grow with me.

3 Moving together, free from fear, with plenteous droppings in this pen,

Bearing sweet milk-like Soma-juice, come hither free from all disease.

4 Come hither, to this place, O Cows: here thrive as though ye were manured.

Even here increase and multiply; let us be friendly, you and me.

5 Auspicious be this stall to you. Prosper like cultivated rice.

Even here increase and multiply. Myself do we bestow on you.

6 Follow me, Cows, as master of the cattle. Here may this Cow- pen make you grow and prosper,

Still while we live may we approach you living, ever increasing with the growth of riches.

HYMN XV

merchant's prayer for success in his business

stir and animate the merchant Indra; may he approach and be our guide and
er.

ng ill-will, wild beast, and highway robber, may he who hath the power
e riches.

ny paths which Gods are wont to travel, the paths which go between the
heaven,

ejoice with me in milk and fatness that I may make rich profit by my

3 With fuel. Agni! and with butter, longing, mine offering I present for strength and conquest;

With prayer, so far as I have strength, adoring—this holy hymn to gain a hundred treasures.

4 Pardon this stubbornness of ours. O Agni, the distant pathway which our feet have trodden.

Propitious unto us be sale and barter, may interchange of merchandise enrich me.

Accept, ye twain, accordant, this libation! Prosperous be our ventures and incomings.

5 The wealth wherewith I carry on my traffic, seeking, ye Gods!

Wealth with the wealth I offer,

May this grow more for me, not less: O Agni, through sacrifice chase those who hinder profit!

6 The wealth wherewith I carry on my traffic, seeking, ye Gods!

Wealth with the wealth I offer,

Herein may Indra, Savitar, and Soma, Prajāpati, and Agni give me splendour.

7 With reverence we sign thy praise, O Hotar-priest Vaisvānara.

Over our children keep thou watch, over our bodies, kine, and lives.

8 Still to thee ever will we bring oblation, as to a stabled horse, O Jātavedas.

Joying in food and in the growth of riches may we thy servants,

Agni, never suffer.

HYMN XVI

A Rishi's morning prayer

1 Agni dat dawn, and Indra we invoke at dawn, and Varuna and Mitra, and the Asvins twain:

Bhaga at dawn, Pūshan and Brāhmanaspati, Soma at dawn, and Rudra we invoke at dawn.

2 We all strong Bhaga, conqueror in the morning, the son of Aditi, the great Disposer,

Whom each who deems himself poor, strong and mighty, a king, addresses thus, Grant thou my portion!

3 Bhaga, our guide, Bhaga whose gifts are faithful, favour this hymn and give us wealth, O Bhaga.

Bhaga, augment our store of kine and horses. Bhaga, may we be rich in men and heroes.

4 So may felicity be ours at present, and when the Sun advances, and at noontide;

And may we still, O Bounteous One, at sunset be happy in the Gods' protecting favour.

5 May Bhaga verily be bliss-bestower, and through him, Gods! May happiness attend us.

As such with all my might I call and call thee: as such be thou our leader here, O Bhaga.

6 To this our sacrifice may the Dawns incline them, and come to the pure place like Dadhikrāvan.

As strong steeds draw a chariot may they bring me hitherward Bhaga who discovers treasure.

7 May the kind Mornings dawn on us for ever with, wealth of kine, of horses, and of heroes.

Streaming with all abundance, pouring fatness,

Do ye preserve us evermore with blessings!

HYMN XVII

A farmer's song and prayer to speed the plough

1 Wise and devoted to the Gods the skilful men bind plough-ropes fast,

And lay the yokes on either side.

2 Lay on the yokes and fasten well the traces: formed is the furrow, sow the seed within it.

Virāj vouchsafe us hearing fraught with plenty!

Let the ripe grain come near and near the sickle.

3 The keen-shared plough that bringeth bliss, furnished with traces and with stilts,

Shear out for me a cow, a sheep, a rapid drawer of the car, a blooming woman, plump and strong!

4 May Indra press the furrow down, may Pūshan guard and cherish her.

May she, well stored with milk yield milk for us through each succeeding year.

5 Happily let the shares turn up the ploughland, the ploughers happily follow the oxen.

Pleased with our sacrifice, Suna and Sira! Make the plants bring this man abundant produce.

6 Happily work our steers and men! May the plough furrow happily.

Happily be the traces bound. Happily ply the driving-goad.

7 Suna and Sira, welcome ye this laud, and with the milk that ye have made in heaven,

Bedew ye both this earth of ours.

8 Auspicious Sitā, come thou near: we venerate and worship thee.

That thou mayst bless and prosper us and bring us fruits abundantly.

9 Loved by the Visvedevas and the Maruts, let Sitā be bedewed with oil and honey.

Turn thou to us with wealth of milk, O Sitā, in vigorous strength and pouring streams of fatness.

BOOK 4

HYMN I

Cosmogonical and mystico-theological doctrine

1 Eastward at first the prayer was generated: Vena disclosed bright flashes from the summit,

Disclosed his deepest, nearest revelations, womb of the non-existent and existent.

2 Let this Queen come in front, her Father's daughter, found in the worlds for earliest generation.

For him they set this radiant vault in motion. Let them prepare warm milk for him who first would drink.

3 He who was born as his all-knowing kinsman declareth all the deities' generations.

He from the midst of prayer his prayer hath taken. On high, below, spread forth his godlike nature.

4 For he, true to the law of Earth and Heaven, established both the mighty worlds securely.

Mighty when born, he propped apart the mighty, the sky, our earthly home, and air's mid-region.

5 He from the depth hath been reborn for ever, Brihaspati the world's sole Lord and Ruler.

From light was born the Day with all its lustre: through this let sages live endowed with splendour.

6 The sage and poet verily advanceth the statute of that mighty God primeval.

He was born here with many more beside him: they slumbered when the foremost side was opened.

7 The man who seeks the friend of Gods, Atharvan the father, and Brihaspati, with worship,

Crying to him, Be thou all things' creator! The wise God, self-dependent, never injures.

Hymn II is missing

HYMN III

A Charm against tigers, wolves, thieves and other noxious creatures

1 Three have gone hence and passed away, the man, the tiger, and the wolf.

Down, verily, the rivers flow, down-goeth the celestial Tree.

Down let our foemen bend and bow.

2 On distant pathway go the wolf, on pathway most remote the thief!

On a far road speed forth the rope with teeth, and the malicious man!

3 We crush and rend to pieces both thine eyes, O Tiger, and thy jaws and all the twenty claws we break.

4 We break and rend the tiger first of creatures that are armed with teeth;

The robber then, and then the snake, the sorcerer, and then the wolf.

5 The thief who cometh near to-day departeth bruised and crushed to bits.

By nearest way let him be gone. Let Indra slay him with his bolt.

6 Let the beast's teeth be broken off, shivered and shattered be his ribs!

Slack be thy bowstring: downward go the wild beast that pursues the hare!

7 Open not what thou hast compressed, close not what thou hast not compressed.

Indra's and Soma's child, thou art Atharvan's tiger-crushing charm.

BOOK 5

HYMN I

A glorification of Trita and Varuna

1 He who with special plans and deathless spirit, waxing, well-born, hath come unto his birth-place,

As he who shines upholds the days, thus Trita, of pure life, bears the Three as their supporter.

2 He who, the first, approached the holy statutes makes, after, many beauteous forms and figures.

Eager to drink, his birth-place first he entered who understands the word when yet unspoken.

3 He who—the fluid gold, with radiant kinsmen—to fervent glow delivered up thy body,

On him both set names, that shall live for ever: to him the regions shall send robes to clothe him,

4 As these have gone to their primeval station, each gaining an imperishable dwelling,

May kissing mothers of the bards' beloved bring the pole-drawing husband to the sister.

5 By holy wisdom I a sage, Far-Strider! Offer to thee this lofty adoration.

This worship both the mighty eddying rivers, coming together to this station, heighten.

6 Seven are the pathways which the wise have fashioned: to one of these may come the troubled mortal.

On sure ground where the ways are parted standeth Life's Pillar in the dwelling of the Highest.

7 Working, I go my way with deathless spirit: life, spirit, bodies have gone gladly thither.

Aye, Sakra also gives his gift of treasure as when the sacrifice meets with power.

8 Yea, the son asks dominion of his father: this they declared the noblest path to welfare.

Varuna, let them see thy revelations: display the wondrous shapes of times to follow.

9 Halt with the milk, its other half, thou minglest and with that half, strong! unbeguiled!

Let us exalt the gracious friend, the mighty, Varuna son of Aditi, strength-giver.

We have told him the marvels sung by poets. The utterance of Heaven and Earth is truthful.

HYMN II

A glorification of Indra

1 In all the worlds that was the best and highest whence sprang the Mighty One of splendid valour.

As soon as born he overcomes his foemen, when those rejoice in him who bring him succour.

2 Grown mighty in his strength, with ample vigour, he as a foe strikes fear into the Dāsa,

Eager to win the breathing and the breathless: All sang thy praise at banquet and oblation.

3 All concentrate on thee their mental vigour what time these, twice or thrice, are thine assistants,

Blend what is sweeter than the sweet with sweetness win quickly with our meath that meath in battle.

4 If verily in every war the sages joy and exult in thee who win treasures,

With mightier power, strong God, extend thy firmness: let not malevolent Kaokas harm thee.

5 Proudly we put our trust in thee in battles, when we behold great wealth the prize of combat.

I with my words impel thy weapons onward, and sharpen with my prayer thy vital vigour.

6 Thou in that house, the highest or the lowest, which thy protection guards, bestowest riches.

Establish ye the ever-wandering mother, and bring full many deeds to their completion.

7 Praise in the height Him who hath many pathways, courageous, strongest, Aptya of the Aptyas

Through strength he shows himself of ample power: pattern of Prithivī, he fights and conquers.

8 Brihaddiva, the foremost of light-winners, hath made these holy prayers, this strength for Indra.

Free Lord, he rules the mighty fold of cattle, winning, aglow, even all the billowy waters.

9 Thus hath Brihaddiva, the great Atharvan, spoken to Indra as himself in person.

Two sisters free from stain, the Mātarivans, with power impel him onward and exalt him.

HYMN III

A prayer to Agni, Indra, and other deities for victory and prosperity

1 Let strength be mine while I invoke thee, Agni! Enkindling thee may we support our bodies.

May the four regions bend and bow before me: with thee for guardian may we win the combat.

2 Baffling the range of our opponents, Agni! Guard us as our protector round about us.

Down the steep slope go they who hate us, backward, and let their thought who watch at home be ruined.

3 May all the Gods be on my side in battle, the Maruts led by Indra, Vishnu, Agni.

Mine be the middle air's extended region, and may the Wind blow favouring these my wishes.

4 For me let them present all mine oblations, and let my mind's intention be accomplished.

May I be guiltless of the least transgression: may all the Gods come hither and protect me.

5 May the Gods grant me riches, may the blessing and invocation of the Gods assist me.

This boon shall the celestial Hotars win us: may we, unwounded, have brave heroes round us.

6 Ye six divine Expanses, give us freedom. Here, all ye Gods, acquit yourselves like heroes.

Let not calamity or curse o'ertake us, nor deeds of wickedness that merit hatred.

7 Do ye three Goddesses give ample shelter and all success to us ourselves and children.

Let us not lose our children or our bodies: let us not benefit the foe, King Soma!

8 Foodful and much-invoked, at this our calling may the far-reaching Bull grant us wide shelter.

Lord of bay coursers, Indra, bless our children: harm us not, give us not as prey to others.

9 Lord of the world, Creator and Disposer, may the God Savitar who quells assailants,

May the Ādityas, Rudras, both the Asvins, Gods, guard the sacrificer from destruction.

10 Let those who are our foemen stay afar from us: with Indra and with Agni we will drive them off.

The Ādityas and the Rudras, over us on high, have made me strong, a thinker, and a sovran lord.

11 Yea, we call Indra hitherward, the winner of wealth in battle and of kine and horses.

May he mark this our worship when we call him, Lord of bay steeds, thou art our friend and comrade.

BOOK 6

HYMN I

In praise of Savitar

1 Sing, Atharvana, at eve, sing loudly, bring a splendid present: hymn God Savitar with praises.

2 Yea, praise him whose home is in the river, Son of Truth, the youthful, gracious friend whose word is guileless.

3 Savitar our God shall send us many everlasting treasures, that both paths may well be travelled.

HYMN II

In praise of Indra

1 For Indra, ministering priests! run ye and press the Soma juice, That he may hear his praiser's word, and this my call.

2 Thou into whom the drops find way as sap pours life into a tree,

Drive off in thine abundant might our demon foes.

3 For Indra, thunder-armed, who drinks the Soma press the Soma out:

He, youthful, conqueror, and Lord is praised by all.

HYMN III

A prayer to various deities for protection and prosperity

1 Guard us the Maruts! Guard us well, O Indra, Piishan, Aditi.

Guard us, O Waters' Child, and Rivers Seven. May Vishnu guard us, and the Sky.

2 May Heaven and Earth take care of us for victory, may Pressing-

Stone and Soma save us from distress.

Sarasvati, auspicious Goddess, guard us well: preserve us Agni and his kind protecting powers.

3 Preserve us both the Asvins, Gods and Lords of Light, and let the Dawns and Night bring us deliverance.

The Waters' Child protect our house from every harm. Do thou,

God Tvashtar, make us strong for health and wealth.

HYMN IV

A hymn to various deities for protection

1 May Tvashtar, Brāhmanaspati, Parjanya hear my holy prayer.

May Aditi with all her sons, the brothers, guard us, invincible, protecting power.

2 May Ansa, Bhaga, Varuna, and Mitra, Aryaman, Aditi, and Maruts guard us.

May we be freed from that oppressor's hatred. May he keep off that foeman who is near us.

3 May both the Asvins further our devotion. With ceaseless care

deliver us, Wide-Ranger! O Father Heaven, keep from us all misfortunes.

HYMN V

A prayer to Agni and Indra for the well-being of a princely patron

1 Agni, adored with sacred oil, lift up this man to high estate.

Endow him with full store of strength and make him rich in progeny.

2 Advance him, Indra! Let him be ruler of all akin to him.

Grant him sufficiency of wealth: guide him to life and length of days.

3 Prosper this man, O Agni, in whose house we offer sacrifice.

May Soma bless him, and the God here present, Brāhmanaspati.

BOOK 7

HYMN I

Glorification of the power of prayer and to Agni

1 They who by thought have guided all that Speech hath best, or
they who with their heart have uttered words of truth,
Made stronger by the strength which the third prayer bestows,
have by the fourth prayer learned the nature of the Cow.
2 Well knows this son his sire, he knows his mother well: he hath
been son, and he hath been illiberal.
He hath encompassed heaven, and air's mid-realm, and sky; he
hath become this All; he hath come nigh to us.

HYMN II

Praise of Atharvan

1 Invoke for us, proclaim in sundry places, the kinsman of the Gods, our sire Atharvan,

His mother's germ, his father's breath, the youthful, who with his mind hath noticed this oblation.

Book 8

HYMN I

A charm to recover a dying man

1 Homage to Death the Ender! May thy breathings, inward and outward, still remain within thee.

Here stay this man united with his spirit in the Sun's realm, the world of life eternal!

2 Bhaga hath lifted up this man, and Soma with his filaments,

Indra and Agni, and the Gods the Maruts, raised him up to health.

3 Here is thy spirit, here thy breath, here is thy life, here is thy soul:

By a celestial utterance we raise thee from Destruction's bonds.

4 Up from this place, O man, rise! Sink not downward, casting away the bonds of Death that hold thee.

Be not thou parted from this world, from sight of Agni and the Sun.

5 Purely for thee breathe Wind and Mātarisvan, and let the Waters rain on thee their nectar.

The Sun shall shine with healing on thy body; Death shall have mercy on thee: do not leave us!

6 Upward must be thy way, O man, not downward: with life and mental vigour I endow thee.

Ascend this car eternal, lightly rolling; then full of years shalt thou address the meeting.

7 Let not thy soul go thither, nor be lost to us: slight not the living, go not where the Fathers are.

Let all the Gods retain thee here in safety.

8 Yearn not for the departed ones, for those who lead men far away.

Rise up from darkness into light: come, both thy hands we
clasp in ours.
9 Let not the black dog and the brindled seize thee, two warders
of the way sent forth by Yama.
Come hither; do not hesitate: with mind averted stay not there.
10 Forbear to tread this path, for it is awful: that path I speak of
which thou hast not travelled.
Enter it not, O man; this way is darkness: forward is danger,
hitherward is safety.
11 Thy guardians be the Fires within the Waters, thy guardian be
the Fire which men enkindle.
Thy guardian be Vaisvānara Jātavedas; let not celestial Fire with
lightning burn thee.
12 Let not the Flesh-Consumer plot against thee: depart thou far
away from the Destroyer.
Be Heaven and Earth and Sun and Moon thy keepers, and from
the dart of Gods may Air protect thee.
13 May Vigilance and Watchfulness protect thee, Sleepless and
Slumberless keep guard above thee!
Let Guardian and let Wakeful be thy warders.
14 Let these be thy preservers, these thy keepers. All hail to these,
to these be lowly worship!
15 May saving Savitar, Vāyu, Indra, Dhātar restore thee to com-
munion with the living.
Let not thy vigour or thy breath forsake thee: we recall thy life.
16 Let not the fiend with snapping jaws, nor darkness find thee:
tongue, holy grass: how shouldst thou perish?

May the Ādityas and the Vasus, Indra and Agni raise thee and
to health restore thee.
17 The Sky hath raised thee, and the Earth, Prajāpati hath raised
thee up.
The Plants and Herbs with Soma as their King have rescued
thee from Death.
18 Here let this man, O Gods, remain: let him not go to yonder
world.
We rescue him from Mrityu with a charm that hath a thousand
powers.
19 I have delivered thee from Death. Strength-givers smelt and
fashion thee!
Let not she-fiends with wild loose locks, or fearful howlers yell
at thee.
20 I have attained and captured thee: thou hast returned restored
to youth.
Perfect in body: so have I found all thy sight and all thy life.
21 Life hath breathed on thee; light hath come: darkness hath past
away from thee.
Far from thee we have buried Death, buried Destruction and:
Decline.

HYMN II

1 Seize to thyself this trust of life for ever: thine be longevity
which nothing shortens.
Thy spirit and thy life again I bring thee: die not, nor vanish

into mist and darkness.

2 Come to the light of living men, come hither: I draw thee to a
life of hundred autumns.
Losing the bonds of Death, the curse that holds thee, I give thee
age of very long duration.
3 Thy breath have I recovered from the Wind, thy vision from the Sun.
Thy mind I stablish and secure within thee: feel in thy members.
Use thy tongue, conversing.
4 I blow upon thee with the breath of bipeds and quadrupeds, as
on a fire new-kindled.
To thee, O Death, and to thy sight and breath have I paid
reverence.
5 Let this man live, let him not die: we raise him, we recover him.
I make for him a healing balm. O Death, forbear to slay this man.
6 Here for sound health I invocate a living animating plant,
Preserving, queller of disease, victorious, full of power and might.
7 Seize him not, but encourage and release him: here let him stay,
though thine, in all his vigour.
Bhava and Sarva, pity and protect him: give him full life and
drive away misfortunes.
8 Comfort him, Death, and pity him: let him arise and pass away,
Unharmed, with all his members, hearing well, with old, may he
through hundred years win profit with his soul.
9 May the Gods' missile pass thee by. I bring thee safe from the
mist: from death have I preserved thee.
Far have I banished flesh-consuming Agni: I place a rampart
for thy life's protection.

10 Saving him from that misty path of thine which cannot be defined.

From that descent of thine, O Death, we make for him a shield of prayer.

11 I give thee both the acts of breath, health, lengthened life, and death by age.

All Yama's messengers who roam around, sent by Vaivasvata,

I chase away.

12 Far off we drive Malignity, Destruction, Pisāchas banqueters on flesh, and Grāhi.

And all the demon kind, the brood of sin, like darkness, we dispel.

13 I win thy life from Agni, from the living everlasting Jātavedas.

This I procure for thee, that thou, undying, mayst not suffer

harm, that thou mayst be content, that all be well with thee.

14 Gracious to thee be Heaven and Earth, bringing no grief, and

drawing nigh!

Pleasantly shine the Sun for thee, the Wind blow sweetly to

thy heart!

Let the celestial Waters full of milk flow happily for thee.

15 Auspicious be the Plants to thee! I have upraised thee, borne

thee from the lower to the upper earth:

Let the two Sons of Aditi, the Sun and Moon, protect thee there.

16 Whatever robe to cover thee or zone thou makest for thyself,

We make it pleasant to thy frame: may it be soft and smooth

to touch.

17 When, with a very keen and cleasing razor, our hair and beards

thou shavest as a barber,

Smoothing our face steal not our vital forces.

18 Auspicious unto thee be rice and barley, causing no painful sick-

ness or consumption, these deliver from calamity.

19 Thy food, thy drink, whate'er they be corn grown by cultivation, milk,
Food eatable, uneatable, I make all poisonless for thee.
20 We give thee over as a charge to Day and Night, in trust to both.
Keep him for me from stingy fiends, from those who fain would feed on him.
21 A hundred, yea, ten thousand years we give thee, ages two, three, four.
May Indra, Agni, all the Gods, with willing favour look on thee.
22 To Autumn we deliver thee, to Winter, Spring and Summer's care.
We trust thee with auspicious years wherein the plants and herbs grow up.
23 Death is the lord of bipeds, Death is sovran lord of quadrupeds.
Away I bear thee from that: Death the ruler: be not thou afraid.
24 Thou, still uninjured, shalt not die: be not afraid; thou shalt not die.
Here where I am men do not die or go to lowest depths of gloom.
25 Here verily all creatures live, the cow, the horse, the man, the beast,
Here where this holy prayer is used, a rampart that protecteth life.
Let it preserve thee from thy peers, from incantation, from thy friends.
26 Live very long, be healthy, be immortal: let not the vital breath
forsake thy body.
27 One and a hundred modes of death, dangers that may be overcome,
May Gods deliver thee from this when Agni, dear to all men, bids.
28 Body of Agni prompt to save, slayer of fiends and foes art thou,
Yea, banisher of malady, the healing balm called Pūtudru.

Book 9

HYMN I

A glorification of the Asvins' whip and a prayer for blessings

1 The Asvins' Honey-whip was born from heaven and earth, from
middle air, and ocean, and from fire and wind.
All living creatures welcome it with joyful hearts, fraught with
the store of Amrit it hath gathered up.
2 They call thee earth's great strength in every form, they call
thee too the ocean's genial seed.
Whence comes the Honey-whip bestowing bounty, there Vital
Spirit is, and Amrit treasured.
3 In sundry spots, repeatedly reflecting, men view upon the earth:
her course and action;
For she, the first-born daughter of the Maruts, derives her
origin from Wind and Agni.
4 Daughter of Vasus, mother of Ādityas, centre of Amrit breath
of living creatures.
The Honey-whip, gold-coloured, dropping fatness, moves as a
mighty embryo 'mid mortals.
5 The deities begat the Whip of Honey: her embryo assumed all
forms and fashions.
The mother nourishes that tender infant which at its birth
looks on all worlds and beings.
6 Who understandeth well, who hath perceived it, her heart's un-
injured Soma-holding beaker?
Let the wise Brāhman priest therein be joyful.
7 He understandeth them, he hath perceived them, her breasts

that pour a thousand streams, uninjured.
They unreluctantly yield strength and vigour.
8 She who with voice upraised in constant clamour, mighty, life-giving, goes unto her function,
Bellowing to the heated three libations, suckles with streams of milk, and still is lowing.
9 On whom, well-fed, the Waters wait in worship, and steers and self-refulgent bulls attend her.
For thee, for one like thee down pour the Waters, and cause desire and strength to rain upon thee.
10 The thunder is thy voice, O Lord of Creatures: a Bull, thou castest on the earth thy vigour.
The Honey-whip, the Manus' first-born daughter, derives her origin from Wind and Agni.
11 As at the morning sacrifice the Asvins twain love Soma well,
Even so may both the Asvins lay splendour and strength within my soul.
12 As at the second sacrifice Indra and Agni love him well,
Let the pair, Indra Agni, lay splendour and strength within my soul.
13 As at third sacrifice Soma is the Ribhus' well-beloved one,
Even so may they, the Ribhus, store splendour and strength within my soul.
14 Fain would I bring forth sweetness, fain would make it mine.
Bringing milk, Agni! Have I come: splendour and strength bestow on me!
15 Grant me, O Agni, splendid strength, and progeny, and length-

ened life.

May the Gods know me as I am, may Indra with the Rishis know.

16 As honey-bees collect and add fresh honey to their honey store,

Even so may both the Asvins lay splendour and strength within my soul.

17 As over honey flies besmear this honey which the bees have made,

So may both Asvins lay in me splendour and strength and power and might.

18 May all the sweetness that is found in hills and mountains, steeds and kine,

And wine that floweth from the cup,—may all that sweetness be in me.

19 May both the Asvins, Lords of Light, balm me with honey of the bees,

That I may speak among the folk words full of splendour and of strength.

20 The thunder is thy voice, O Lord of Creatures: a Bull, thou castest strength on earth and heaven.

To that all cattle look for their existence: with this she nourishes their force and vigour.

21 The Whip itself is Heaven, Earth is the handle, the point of juncture is the Air's mid-region.

The lash is lightning, and the tip is golden.

22 Whoever knows the Whip's seven kinds of honey, becomes himself a man endowed with sweetness.

Brāhman and King, the draught-ox and the milch-cow, barley
and rice, and honey is the seventh.
23 Sweet is the man, sweet are his goods and chattels: he who
knows this conquers the worlds of sweetness.
24 The thundering of Prajāpati in heaven is verily manifest to living creatures.
Therefore I stand from right to left invested, and, O Prajāpati,
I cry, regard me!
The man who hath this knowledge is regarded by living beings
and the Lord of Creatures.

HYMN II

A glorification of Kāma as God of desire of all that is good
1 Kāma the Bull, slayer of foes, I worship with molten butter, sacrifice, oblation.
Beneath my feet cast down mine adversaries with thy great
manly power, when I have praised thee.
2 That which is hateful to mine eye and spirit, that harasses and
robs me of enjoyment,
The evil dream I loose upon my foemen. May I rend him when
I have lauded Kāma.
3 Kāma, do thou, a mighty Lord and Ruler, let loose ill dream,
misfortune, want of children,
Homelessness, Kāma! Utter destitution, upon the sinner who
designs my ruin.
4 Drive them away, drive them afar, O Kāma; indigence fall on
those who are my foemen!
When they have been cast down to deepest darkness, consume
their dwellings with thy fire, O Agni.

5 She, Kāma! She is called the Cow, thy daughter, she who is
named Vāk and Virāj by sages.
By her drive thou my foemen to a distance. May cattle, vital
breath, and life forsake them.
6 By Kāma's might, King Varuna's and Indra's, by Vishnu's
strength, and Savitar's instigation,
I chase my foes with sacrifice to Agni, as a deft steersman drives
his boat through waters.
7 May Kāma, mighty one, my potent warder, give me full free-
dom from mine adversaries.
May all the Deities be my protection, all Gods come nigh to
this mine invocation.
8 Accepting this oblation rich with fatness, be joyful here, ye
Gods whose chief is Kāma,
Giving me freedom from mine adversaries.
9 Ye, Indra, Agni, Kāma! Come together and cast mine adver-
saries down beneath me.
When they have sunk into the deepest darkness, O Agni, with
thy fire consume their dwellings.
10 Slay those who are mine enemies, O Kāma: headlong to depth
of blinding darkness hurl them.
Reft be they all of manly strength and vigour! Let them not
have a single day's existence.
11 Kāma hath slain those who were mine opponents, and given me
ample room to grow and prosper.
Let the four regions bow them down before me, and let the
six expanses bring me fatness.
12 Let them drift downward like a boat torn from the rope that

held it fast.
There is no turning back for those whom our keen arrows have repelled.
13 Agni averts, Indra averts, and Soma: may the averting Gods avert this foeman.
14 To be avoided by his friends, detested, repelled, with few men round him, let him wander.
Yea, on the earth descend the lightning-flashes: may the strong God destroy your adversaries.
15 This potent lightning nourishes things shaken, and things unshaken yet, and all the thunders.
May the Sun, rising with his wealth and splendour, drive in victorious might my foemen downward.
16 Thy firm and triply-barred protection, Kāma! thy spell, made weapon-proof extended armour
With that drive thou my foemen to a distance. May cattle, vital breath, and life forsake them.
17 Far from the world wherein we live, O Kāma, drive thou my foemen with that selfsame weapon
Wherewith the Gods repelled the fiends, and Indra cast down the Dasyus into deepest darkness.
18 As Gods repelled the Asuras, and Indra down to the lowest darkness drove the demons,
So, Kāma, from this world, to distant places, drive thou the men who are mine adversaries.
19 First before all sprang Kāma into being. Gods, Fathers, mortal men have never matched him.
Stronger than these art thou, and great for ever. Kāma, to thee,

to thee I offer worship.
20 Wide as the space which heaven and earth encompass, far as
the flow of waters, far as Agni,
Stronger than these art thou, and great for ever. Kāma, to thee,
to thee I offer worship.
21 Vast as the quarters of the sky and regions that lie between
them spread in all directions, vast as celestial tracts and views
of heaven,
Stronger than these art thou, and great for ever. Kāma, to thee,
to thee I offer worship.
22 Many as are the bees, and bats, and reptiles, and female serpents
of the trees, and beetles,
Stronger art thou than these, and great for ever. Kāma, to thee,
to thee I offer worship.
23 Stronger art thou than aught that stands or twinkles, stronger
art thou than ocean, Kāma! Manyu!
Stronger than these art thou, and great for ever. Kāma, to thee,
to thee I offer worship.
24 Not even Vāta is the peer of Kāma, not Agni, Chandramas
the Moon, nor Sūrya.
Stronger than these art thou, and great for ever. Kāma, to thee,
to thee I offer worship.
25 Thy lovely and auspicious forms, O Kāma, whereby the thing
thou wilt becometh real,
With these come thou and make thy home among us, and make
malignant thoughts inhabit elsewhere.

Book 10

HYMN I

A charm against witchcraft

1 Afar let her depart: away we drive her whom, made with hands, all-beautiful,

Skilled men prepare and fashion like a bride amid her nuptial train.

2 Complete, with head and nose and ears, all-beauteous, wrought with magic skill

Afar let her depart: away we drive her.

3 Made by a Sidra or a Prince, by priests or women let her go.

Back to her maker as her kin, like a dame banished by her lord.

4 I with this salutary herb have ruined all their magic arts,

The spell which they have cast upon thy field, thy cattle, or thy men.

5 I'll fall on him who doeth ill, on him who curseth fall the curse!

We drive her back that she may slay the man who wrought the witchery.

6 Against her comes the Angirasa, the Priest whose eye is over us.

Turn back all witcheries and slay those practisers of magic arts.

7 Whoever said to thee, Go forth against the foeman up the stream,

To him, O Krityā, go thou back. Pursue not us, the sinless ones.

8 He who composed thy limbs with thought as a deft joiner builds a car,

Go to him: thither lies thy way. This man is all unknown to
thee.
9 The cunning men, the sorcerers who fashioned thee and held thee
fast,—
This cures and mars their witchery, th''''s, repellent, drives it back
the way it came. With this we make thee swim.
10 When we have found her ducked and drenched, a hapless cow
whose calf hath died,
Let all my woe depart and let abundant riches come to me.
11 If, as they gave thy parents aught, they named thee, or at sacri-
fice,
From all their purposed evil let these healing herbs deliver thee.
12 From mention of thy name, from sin against the Fathers or the
Gods,
These herbs of healing shall by prayer release thee, by power,
by holy texts, the milk of .Rishis.
13 As the wind stirs the dust from earth and drives the rain cloud
from the sky,
So, chased and banished by the spell, all misery departs from
me.
14 Go with a resonant cry, depart, like a she-ass whose cords are
loosed.
Go to thy makers: hence! Away! Go driven by the potent
spell.
15 This, Krityā, is thy path, we say, and guide thee. We drive thee
back who hast been sent against us.
Go by this pathway, breaking loose for onslaught even as a host

complete with cars and horses.

16 No path leads hitherward for thee to travel. Turn thee from us:
far off, thy light is yonder.
Fly hence across the ninety floods, the rivers most hard to pass.
Begone, and be not wounded.

17 As wind the trees, so smite and overthrow them: leave not cow,
horse, or man of them surviving
Return, O Krityā, unto those who made thee. Wake them from
sleep to find that they are childless.

18 The charm or secret power which they have buried for thee in
sacred grass, field, cemetery,
Or spell in household fire which men more cunning have
wrought against thee innocent and simple,—

19 That tool of hatred, understood, made ready, stealthy and buried
deep, have we discovered, p. 3
Let that go back to whence it came, turn thither like a horse
and kill the children of the sorcerer.

20 Within our house are swords of goodly iron. Krityā, we know
thy joints and all their places.
Arise this instant and begone! What, stranger! Art thou seek-
ing here?

21 O Krityā, I will cut thy throat and hew thy feet off. Run, be-
gone!
Indra and Agni, Guardian Lords of living creatures, shield us
well!

22 May Soma, gracious friend, imperial Sovran, and the world's
Masters look on us with favour.

23 Bhava and Sarva cast the flash of lightning, the weapon of the
Gods, against the sinner who made the evil thing, who deals
in witchcraft!
24 If thou hast come two-footed or four-footed, made by the
sorcerer, wrought in perfect beauty,
Become eight-footed and go hence. Speed back again, thou evil
one.
25 Anointed, balmed, and well adorned, bearing all trouble with
thee, go.
Even as a daughter knows her sire, so know thy marker, Krityā,
thou.
26 Krityā, begone, stay not. Pursue as 'twere the wounded crea-
ture's track.
He is the chase, the hunter thou he may not slight or humble thee.
27 He waits, and aiming with his shaft smites him who first would
shoot at him,
And, when the foeman deals a blow before him, following strikes
him down.
28 Hearken to this my word; then go thither away whence thou
hast come; to him who made thee go thou back.
29 The slaughter of an innocent, O Krityā, is an awful deed. Slay
not cow, horse, or man of ours.
In whatsoever place thou art concealed we rouse thee up there-
from: become thou lighter than a leaf.
30 If ye be girt about with clouds of darkness, bound as with a
net.
We rend and tear all witcheries hence and to their maker send

them back.

31 The brood of wizard, sorcerer, the purposer of evil deed.
Crush thou, O Krityā spare not, kill those practisers of magic arts.

32 As Sūrya frees himself from depth of darkness, and casts away the night and rays of morning,
So I repel each baleful charm which an enchanter hath prepared;
And, as an elephant shakes off the dust, I cast the plague aside.

Book 11

HYMN I

An accompaniment to the preparation and presentation of a Brahmaudana

1 Agni, spring forth! Here Aditi, afflicted, cooks a Brahmaudana,
yearning for children.
Let the Seven Rishis, World-creators, rub thee into existence
here with gift of offspring.
2 Raise, as I bid, the smoke, my strong companions, lovers of free-
dom from deceit and malice!
Victor in fight heroic, here is Agni by whom the Gods subdued
the hostile demons.
3 Thou, Agni, wart produced for mighty valour, to cook Brahmau-
dana, O Jātavedas.
Seven Rishis, makers of the world, begat thee, Grant to this
woman wealth with store of heroes.
4 Burn up, O Agni, kindled with the fuel. Knowing the Gods who
merit worship, bring them.
Cooking, for these, oblation, Jātavedas! Lift up this man to
heaven's most lofty summit.
5 Your portion from of old is triply parted, portion of Gods, of
Fathers, and of mortals.
Know, all, your shares. I deal them out among you. The portion
of the Gods shall save this woman.
6 Strong art thou, Agni, conquering, all-surpassing. Crush down
our foemen, ruin those who hate us.
So let this measure, measured, being measured, make all our kin
thy tributary vassals.

7 Increase with kinsmen and with all abundance: to mighty strength
and power lift up this woman.
Erect, rise upward to the sky's high station, rise to the lofty
world which men call Svarga.
8 May this great Earth receive the skin, this Goddess Prithivī,
showing us her love and favour. Then may we go unto the
world of virtue.
9 Fix on the skin these two joined press-stones, duly rending the
fibres for the sacrificer.
Strike down and slay those who assail this woman, and elevating
raise on high her offspring.
10 Grasp with thy hand, O man, the well-formed press-stones: the
holy Gods have come unto thy worship.
Three wishes of thy heart which thou electest, these happy gains
for thee I here make ready.
11 Here thy devotion is, here is thy birthplace. Aditi, Mother of
brave sons, accept thee!
Wipe away those who fight against this woman with wealth and
store of goodly sons endow her.
12 Rest in the roaring frame of wood: be parted from husk and
chaff, ye Sacrificial Fibres.
May we surpass in glory all our rivals. I cast beneath my feet
the men who hate us.
13 Go, Dame, and quickly come again: the waters, enclosed, have
mounted thee that thou mayst bear them.
Take thou of these such as are fit for service: skilfully separating.
leave the others.

14 Hither these Dames have come in radiant beauty. Arise and seize=
upon thy strength, O woman.
To thee hath sacrifice come: take the pitcher, blest with a good
lord, children, children's children.
15 Instructed by the Rishis, bring those waters, the share of strength
which was of old assigned you.
Let this effectual sacrifice afford you protection, fortune, off-
spring, men, and cattle.
16 Agni, on thee the sacrificial caldron hath mounted: shining,.
fiercely flaming, heat it.
May hottest flames, divine, sprung from the Rishis, gathering,
with the Seasons, heat this portion.
17 Purified, bright, and holy, let these Women, these lucid waters
glide into the caldron.
Cattle and many children may they give us. May he who cooks.
the Odana go to heaven.
18 Ye, Sacrificial Rice and Soma Fibres, cleansed and made pure by
prayer and molten butter.
Enter the water: let the caldron take you. May he who dresses
this ascend to heaven.
19 Expand thyself abroad in all thy greatness, with thousand Prish-
thas, in the world of virtue.
Grandfathers, fathers, children, and descendants, fifteenth am I
to thee when I have dressed it.
20 With thousand streams and Prishthas, undecaying, Brahmaudana
is celestial, God-reaching.
Those I give up to thee with all their children. Force them to

tribute, but to me be gracious.

21 Rise to the altar: bless this dame with offspring. Promote this
woman; drive away the demons.
May we surpass in glory all our rivals. I cast beneath my feet the
men who hate us.

22 Approach this woman here with store of cattle: together with
the deities come to meet her.
Let not a curse or imprecation reach thee: in thine own seat
shine forth exempt from sickness.

23 Fashioned at first by Right, set by the spirit, this altar of Brahmau-
dana was appointed.
Place the pure boiler on it, woman! Set thou therein the rice
mess of Celestial Beings.

24 This second hand of Aditi, this ladle which the Seven Rishis,
world-creators, fashioned.
May this scoop deftly pile upon the altar, therein, the members
of the rice-oblation.

25 Let the dressed offering and divine Ones serve thee: creep from.
the fire again, own these as masters.
Made pure with Soma rest within the Brāhmans: let not thine
eaters, Rishis' sons, be injured.

26 Give understanding unto these, King Soma! all the good Brāh
mans who attend and serve thee.
Oft, in Brahmaudana, and well I call on: Rishis, their sons, and
those who sprang from Fervour.

27 Here I set singly in the hands of Brāhmans these cleansed and.
purifie d and holy Women,

May Indra, Marut girt, grant me the blessing which as I sprinkle you, my heart desireth.

28 Here is my gold, a light immortal: ripened grain from the field this Cow of Plenty give me!

This wealth I place among the Brāhmans, making a path that leads to heaven among the Fathers.

29 Lay thou the chaff in Agni Jātavedas: remove the husks and drive them to a distance.

That, we have heard, that is the House-Lord's portion: we know the share allotted to Destruction.

30 Mark him who toils and cooks and pours oblation: make this man climb the path that leads to heaven,

That he may mount and reach life that is highest, ascending to the loftiest vault above us.

31 Adhvaryu, cleanse that face of the Supporter. Make room, well knowing, for the molten butter.

Purify duly all the limbs with fatness. I make a path to heaven amid the Fathers.

32 Supporter, send to those men fiends and battle, to all non-Brahmans who attend and serve thee.

Famous and foremost, with their great possessions, let not these here, the Rishis sons, be injured.

33 I set thee, Odana, with Rishis' children: naught here belongs to men not sprung from Rishis.

Let Agni my protector, all the Maruts, the Visve Devas guard the cooked oblation.

34 May we adore thee, Sacrifice that yieldeth an everlasting son,

cow, home of treasures,

Together with increasing store of riches, long life and immortality of children.

35 Thou art a Bull that mounts to heaven: to Rishis and their offspring go.

Rest in the world of pious men: there is the place prepared for us.

36 Level the ways: go thitherward, O Agni. Make ready thou the Godward-leading pathways.

By these our pious actions may we follow sacrifice dwelling in the seven-rayed heaven.

37 May we invested with that light go upward, ascending to the sky's most lofty summit.

Wherewith the Gods, what time they had made ready Brahmaudana, mounted to the world of virtue.

HYMN II

Prayer and praise to Bhava, Sarva and Rudra

1 Bhava and Sarva, spare us, be not hostile. Homage to you, twin Lords of beasts and spirits!

Shoot not the arrow aimed and drawn against us: forbear to harm our quadrupeds and bipeds.

2 Cast not our bodies to the dog or jackal, nor, Lord of Beasts! to carrion-kites or vultures.

Let not thy black voracious flies attack them; let not thy birds obtain them for their banquet.

3 We offer homage to thy shout, Bhava! thy breath, thy racking pains:

Homage, Immortal One! to thee, to Rudra of the thousand eyes.

4 We offer reverence to thee from eastward, and from north and south,

From all the compass of the sky, to thee and to the firmament.

5 Homage, O Bhava, Lord of Beasts, unto thy face and all thine eyes,

To skin, and hue, and aspect, and to thee when looked at from behind!

6 We offer homage to thy limbs, thy belly, and thy tongue, and mouth we offer homage to thy smell.

7 Never may we contend with him, the mighty archer, thousand-eyed.

Rudra who wears black tufts of hair, the slaughterer of Ardhaka.

8 May he, may Bhava from all sides avoid us, avoid us even as fire avoids the waters. Let him not threaten us. To him be homage!

9 Four times, eight times be homage paid to Bhava, yea, Lord of Beasts, ten times be reverence paid thee!

Thine are these animals, five several classes, oxen, and goats and sheep, and men, and horses

10 Thine the four regions, thine are earth and heaven, thine, Mighty One, this firmament between them;

Thine everything with soul and breath here on the surface of the

land.
11 Thine is this ample wealth-containing storehouse that holds with-
in it all these living creatures.
Favour us, Lord of Beasts, to thee be homage! Far from us go
ill-omens, dogs, and jackals, and wild-haired women with
their horrid shrieking!
12 A yellow bow of gold thou wieldest, slaying its hundred, tufted
God! smiting its thousand.
Weapon of Gods, far flies the shaft of Rudra: wherever it may
be, we pay it homage.
13 Thou, Rudra, followest close the foe who lies in wait to conquer
thee.
Even as a hunter who pursues the footsteps of the wounded
game.
14 Accordant and allies, Bhava and Rudra, with mighty strength ye
go to deeds of valour. Wherever they may be, we pay them
homage.
15 Be homage, Rudra, unto thee approaching and departing hence!
Homage to thee when standing still, to thee when seated and at
rest!
16 Homage at evening and at morn, homage at night, homage by
day.
To Bhava and to Sarva, both, have I paid lowly reverence,
17 Let us not outrage with our tongue far-seeing Rudra, thousand-
eyed,
Inspired with varied lore, who shoots his arrows forward, far
away.

18 Foremost we go to meet his car, the chariot of the long-haired
God,
Drawn by brown horses, dusky, black, o'erthrowing, slaying,
terrible. Let reverence be paid to him.
19 Cast not thy club at us, thy heavenly weapon. Lord of Beasts,
be not wroth with us. Let reverence be paid to thee.
Shake thy celestial branch above some others elsewhere, not o'er
us.
20 Do us no harm, but comfort us: avoid thou us, and be not
wroth. Never let us contend with thee.
21 Covet not thou our kine or men, covet not thou our goats or
sheep.
Elsewhither, strong One! turn thine aim: destroy the mockers'
family.
22 Homage to him whose weapon, Cough or Fever, assails one like
the neighing of a stallion; to him who draws one forth and
then another!
23 Homage be paid him with ten Sakvari verses who stands
established in the air's mid-region, slaying non-sacrificing
God-despisers!
24 For thee were forest beasts and sylvan creatures placed in the
wood, and small birds, swans, and eagles.
Floods, Lord of Beasts! contain thy living beings: to swell thy
strength flow the celestial Waters.
25 Porpoises, serpents, strange aquatic monsters, fishes, and things
unclean at which thou shootest.
Nothing is far for thee, naught checks thee, Bhava! The whole

earth in a moment thou surveyest. From the east sea thou smitest in the northern.
26 O'erwhelm us not with Fever or with poison, nor, Rudra! With the fire that comes from heaven. Elsewhere, and not on us, cast down this lightning.
27 Ruler of heaven and Lord of earth is Bhava: Bhava hath filled the spacious air's mid-region. Where'er he be, to him be paid our homage!
28 King Bhava, favour him who offers worship, for thou art Pasupati, Lord of victims.
Be gracious to the quadruped and biped of the believer in the Gods' existence.
29 Harm thou among us neither great nor little, not one who bears us, not our future bearers.
Injure no sire among us, harm no mother. Forbear to injure our own bodies, Rudra.
30 This lowly reverence have I paid to Rudra's dogs with mighty mouths,
Hounds terrible with bark and howl, who gorge unmasticated food.
31 Homage to thy loud-shouting hosts and thy long-haired followers!
Homage to hosts that are adored, homage to armies that enjoy
Homage to all thy troops, O God. Security and bliss be ours!

SAM VEDA

PART FIRST

BOOK I
CHAPTER I

Om. Glory to the Samaveda! To Lord Ganesa glory! Om.

DECADE I Agni

1. Come, Agni, praised with song, to feast and sacrificial offering: sit
As Hotar on the holy grass!
2. O Agni, thou hast been ordained Hotar of every sacrifice,
By Gods, among the race of men.
3. Agni we choose as envoy, skilled performer of this holy rite,
Hotar, possessor of all wealth.
4. Served with oblation, kindled, bright, through love of song may Agni, bent
On riches, smite the Vritras dead!
5. I laud your most beloved guest like a dear friend, O Agni, him
Who, like a chariot, wins us wealth.
6. Do thou, O Agni, with great might guard us from all malignity,
Yea, from the hate of mortal man!
7. O Agni, come; far other songs of praise will I sing forth to thee.
Wax mighty with these Soma-drops!
8. May Vatsa draw thy mind away even from thy loftiest dwelling place!
Agni, I yearn for thee with song.
9. Agni, Atharvan brought thee forth by rubbing from the sky, the head
Of all who offer sacrifice.
10. O Agni, bring us radiant light to be our mighty succour, for
Thou art our visible deity!

DECADE II Agni

1. O Agni, God, the people sing reverent praise to thee for strength:

With terrors trouble thou the foe

2. I seek with song your messenger, oblation-bearer, lord of wealth,

Immortal, best at sacrifice.

3. Still turning to their aim in thee the sacrificer's sister hymns

Have come to thee before the wind.

4. To thee, illuminer of night, O Agni, day by day with prayer,

Bringing thee reverence, we come.

5. Help, thou who knowest lauds, this work, a lovely hymn in Rudra's praise,

Adorable in every house!

6. To this fair sacrifice to drink the milky draught art thou called forth:

O Agni, with the Maruts come!

7. With homage will I reverence thee, Agni, like a long-tailed steed,

Imperial lord of holy rites.

8. As Aurva and as Bhrigu called, as Apnavana called, I call

The radiant Agni robed with sea.

9. When he enkindles Agni, man should with his heart attend the song:

I kindle Agni till he glows.

10. Then, verily, they see the light refulgent of primeval seed,

Kindled on yonder side of heaven.

DECADE III Agni

1. Hither, for powerful kinship, I call Agni, him who prospers you,

Most frequent at our solemn rites.

2. May Agni with his pointed blaze cast down each fierce devouring fiend:

May Agni win us wealth by war!

3. Agni, be gracious; thou art great: thou hast approached the pious man,

Hast come to sit on sacred grass.

4. Agni, preserve us,from distress consume our enemies, O God,

Eternal, with thy hottest flames

5. Harness, O Agni, O thou God, thy steeds which are most excellent!

The fleet ones bring thee rapidly.

6. Lord of the tribes, whom all must seek, we worshipped Agni set thee down,

Refulgent, rich in valiant men.

7. Agni is head and height of heaven, the master of the earth is he

He quickeneth the waters' seed.

8. O Agni, graciously announce this our good fortune of the Gods,

And this our newest hymn of praise!

9, By song, O Agni, Angiras! Gopavana hath brought thee forth

Hear thou my call, refulgent one!

10. Agni, the Sage, the Lord of Strength, hath moved around the sacred gifts,

Giving the offerer precious things.

11. His heralds bear him up aloft, the God who knoweth all that lives,

The Sun, that all may look on him.

12, Praise Agni in the sacrifice, the Sage whose holy laws are true

The God who driveth grief away.

13. Kind be the Goddesses to lend us help, and kind that we may drink:

May their streams bring us health and wealth

14. Lord of the brave, whose songs dost thou in thine abundance now inspire,

Thou whose hymns help to win the kine?

DECADE IV Agni

1. Sing to your Agni with each song, at every sacrifice for strength.

Come, let us praise the wise and, everlasting God even as a well-beloved friend,

2. Agni, protect thou us by one, protect us by the second song,

Protect us by three hymns, O Lord of power and might, bright God, by four hymns guard us well!

3. O Agni, with thy lofty beams, with thy pure brilliancy, O God,

Kindled, most youthful one! by Bharadvaja's hand, shine on us richly, holy Lord!

4. O Agni who art worshipped well, dear let our princes be to thee,

Our wealthy patrons who are governors of men, who part, as gifts, the stall of kine!

5. Agni, praise-singer! Lord of men, God! burning up the Rakshasas,

Mighty art thou, the ever-present, household-lord! home-friend and guardian from the sky.

6. Immortal Jatavedas, thou bright-hued refulgent gift of Dawn,

Agni, this day to him who pays oblations bring the Gods who waken with the morn!

7. Wonderful, with thy favouring help, send us thy bounties, gracious Lord.

Thou art the charioteer, Agni, of earthly wealth: find rest and safety for our seed!

8. Famed art thou, Agni, far and wide, preserver, righteous, and a Sage.

The holy singers, O enkindled radiant one, ordainers, call on thee to come.

9. O holy Agni, give us wealth famed among men and strengthening life!

Bestow on us, O helper, that which many crave, more glorious still through righteousness!

10. To him, who dealeth out all wealth, the sweet-toned Hotar-priest of men,

To him like the first vessels filled with savoury juice, to Agni let the lauds go forth.

DECADE V Agni

1. With this mine homage I invoke Agni for you, the Son of Strength,

Dear, wisest envoy, skilled in noble sacrifice, immortal messenger of all.

2. Thou liest in the logs that are thy mothers: mortals kindle thee.

Alert thou bearest off the sacrifleer's gift, and then thou shinest to the Gods.

3. He hath appeared, best prosperer, in whom men lay their holy acts:

So may our songs of praise come nigh to Agni who was born to give the Arya strength!

4. Chief Priest is Agni at the laud, as stones and grass at sacrifice.

Gods! Maruts! Brahmanaspati! I crave with song the help that is most excellent.

5. Pray Agni of the piercing flame, with sacred songs, to be our help;

For wealth, famed Agni, Purumilha and ye men! He is Suditi's sure defence.

6. Hear, Agni who hast ears to hear, with all thy train of escort Gods!

With those who come at dawn let Mitra, Aryaman sit on the grass at sacrifice.

7. Agni of Divodasa, God, comes forth like Indra in his might.

Rapidly hath he moved along his mother earth: he stands in high heaven's dwelling-place.

8. Whether thou come from earth or from the lofty lucid realm of heaven,

Wax stronger in thy body through my song of praise: fill full all creatures, O most wise!

9. If, loving well the forests, thou wentest to thy maternal floods,

Not to be scorned, Agni, is that return of thine when, from afar, thou now art here.

10. O Agni, Manu stablished thee a light for all the race of men:

With Kanva hast thou blazed, Law-born and waxen strong, thou whom the people reverence.

CHAPTER II

DECADE I Agni

1. The God who giveth wealth accept your full libation poured to, him!

Pour ye it out, then fill the vessel full again, for so the God regardeth you.

2. Let Brahmanaspati come forth, let Sunrita the Goddess come,

And Gods bring to our rite which yields a fivefold gift the hero, lover of mankind!

3. Stand up erect to lend us aid, stand up like Savitar the God,

Erect as strength-bestower when we call on thee with priests who balm our offerings!

4. The man who bringeth gifts to thee, bright God who fain wouldst lead to wealth,

Winneth himself a brave son, Agni! skilled in lauds, one prospering in a thousand ways.

5. With hymns and holy eulogies we supplicate your Agni, Lord

Of many families who duly serve the Gods, yea, him whom others too inflame.

6. This Agni is the Lord of great prosperity and hero, strength,

Of wealth with noble offspring and with store of kine, the Lord of battles with the foe.

7. Thou, Agni, art the homestead's Lord, our Hotar-priest at sacrifice.

Lord of all boons, thou art the Potar, passing wise. Pay worship, and enjoy the good!

8. We as thy friends have chosen thee, mortals a God, to be our help.

The Waters' Child, the blessed, the most mighty one, swift conqueror, and without a peer.

DECADE II Agni

1. Present oblations, make him splendid: set ye as Hotar in his place the Home's Lord, worshipped

With gifts and homage where they pour libations! Honour him meet for reverence in our houses.

2. Verily wondrous is the tender youngling's growth who never draweth nigh to drink his mother's milk.

As soon as she who hath no udder bore him, he, faring on his. great errand, suddenly grew strong.

3. Here is one light for thee, another yonder: enter the third and, be therewith united.

Beautiful be thy union with the body, beloved in the Gods' sublimest birthplace!

4. For Jatavedas, worthy of our praise, will we frame with our mind this eulogy as 'twere a car;

For good, in his assembly, is this care of ours. Let us not, in thy friendship, Agni, suffer harm!

5. Agni Vaisvanara, born in course of Order, the messenger of earth, the head of heaven,

The Sage, the sovran, guest of men, our vessel fit for their mouth, the Gods have generated.

6. Even as the waters from the mountain ridges, so sprang the; Gods, through lauds, from thee, O Agni.

To thee speed hymns and eulogies, as horses haste, bearing him who loves the song, to battle.

7. Win to protect you, Rudra, lord of worship, priest of both worlds, effectual sacrificer,

Agni, invested with his golden colours, before the thunder strike and lay you senseless!

8. The King whose face is decked with oil is kindled with homage offered by his faithful servant.

The men, the priests adore him with oblations. Agni hath shone forth at the flush of morning.

9. Agni advanceth with his lofty banner: through earth and heaven the Bull hath loudly bellowed

He hath come nigh from the sky's farthest limit: the Steer hath waxen in the waters' bosom.

10. From the two fire-sticks have the men engendered with thoughts, urged by the hand, the glorious Agni,

Far-seen, with pointed flame, Lord of the Homestead.

DECADE III Agni

1. Agni is wakened by the people's fuel to meet the Dawn who cometh like a milch-cow.

Like young trees shooting up on high their branches, his flames are mounting to the vault of heaven.

2. Set forth the gleaming one, the song-inspirer, not foolish with the foolish, fort-destroyer,

Who leadeth with his hymns to thought of conquest, gold-bearded, richly splendid with his armour

3. Thou art like heaven: one form is bright, one holy, like Day and Night dissimilar in colour.

All magic powers thou aidest, self-dependent! Auspicious bethy bounty here, O Pushan!

4. As holy food, Agni, to thine invoker give wealth in cattle, lasting, rich in marvels!

To us be born a son and spreading offspring. Agni, be this thy gracious will to us-ward!

5. Stablished to fill the juice with vital vigour, giver of wealth, guard of his servant's body,

The great Priest, born, who knows the clouds, abider with men, is seated in the waters' eddy.

6. Let the song, honouring the best, with longing honour the Asura's most famous sovran,

The deeds of him the mighty, deeds like Indra's, the manly one in whom the folk must triumph!

7. In the two kindling-blocks lies Jatavedas like the well-cherished germ in pregnant women,--

Agni who day by day must be entreated by men who watch provided with oblations.

8. Agni, from days of old thou slayest demons: never shall Rakshasas in fight o'ercome thee.

Burn up the foolish ones, raw flesh devourers: let none of them escape thine heavenly arrow!

DECADE IV Agni

1. Bring us most mighty splendour thou, Agni, resistless on thy way:

Prepare for us the path that leads to glorious opulence and strength!

2. May the brave man, if full of zeal he serve and kindle Agni's flame,

Duly presenting sacred gifts, enjoy the Gods' protecting help.

3. Thy bright smoke lifts itself aloft, and far-extended shines in heaven,

For, Purifier! like the Sun thou beamest with thy radiant glow.

4. Thou, Agni, even as Mitra, hast a princely glory of thine own.

Bright, active God, thou makest fame increase like means of nourishment.

5. At dawn let Agni, much-beloved, guest of the house, be glorified,

In whom, the everlasting one, all mortals make their offerings blaze.

6. Most moving song be Agni's: shine on high, O rich in radiant light!

Like the chief consort of a King riches and strength proceed from thee.

7. Exerting all our strength with thoughts of power we glorify in speech

Agni your dear familiar friend, the darling guest in every house.

8. His beam hath lofty power of life: sing praise to Agni, to the God

Whom men have set in foremost place, like Mitra for their eulogy!

9. To noblest Agni, friend of man, chief Vritra-slayer, have we come-

Who with Srutarvan, Riksha's son, in lofty presence is inflamed.

10. Born as the loftiest Law commands, comrade of those who grew with him.

Agni, the sire of Kasyapa by faith, the mother, Manu, Sage.

DECADE V Agni

1. We in King Soma place our trust, in Agni, and in Varuna,

The Aditya, Vishnu, Surya, and the Brahman-priest Brihaspati.

2. Hence have these men gone up on high and mounted to the heights of heaven:

On! conquer on the path by which Angirasas travelled to the skies!

3. That thou mayst send us ample wealth, O Agni, we will kindler thee:

So, for the great oblation, Steer, pray Heaven and Earth to come to us!

4. He runs when one calls after him, This is the prayer of him who prays.

He holds all knowledge in his grasp even as the felly rounds the wheel.

5. Shoot forth, O Agni, with thy flame: demolish them on every side!

Break down the Yatudhana's strength, the vigour of the Rakshasa!

6. Worship the Vasus, Agni! here, the Rudras and Adityas, all

Who know fair sacrifices, sprung from Mann, scattering blessings down!

BOOK II

CHAPTER I

DECADE I Agni

1. Agni, thy faithful servant I call upon thee with many a gift,

As in the keeping of the great inciting God.

2. To Agni, to the Hotar-priest offer your best, your lofty speech,

To him ordainer-like who bears the light of songs.

3. O Agni, thou who art the lord of wealth in kine, thou Son of Strength,

Bestow on us, O Jatavedas, high renown

4. Most skilled in sacrifice, bring the Gods, O Agni, to the pious, man:

A joyful Priest, thy splendour drives our foes afar

5. Taught by seven mothers at his birth was he, for glory of the wise.

He, firm and sure, hath set his mind on glorious wealth

6. And in the day our prayer is this: May Aditi come nigh to help,

With loving-kindness bring us weal and chase our foes

7. Worship thou Jatavedas, pray to him who willingly accepts,

Whose smoke wanders at will, and none may grasp his flame

8. No mortal man can e'er prevail by arts of magic over him

Who hath served Agni well, the oblation-giving God.

9. Agni, drive thou the wicked foe, the evil-hearted thief away,

Far, far, Lord of the brave! and give us easy paths!

10. O hero Agni, Lord of men, on hearing this new laud of mine

Burn down the Rakshasas, enchanters, with thy flame!

DECADE II Agni

1. Sing forth to him the holy, most munificent, sublime with his refulgent glow,

To Agni, ye Upastutas

2. Agni, he conquers by thine aid that brings him store of valiant sons and does great deeds,

Whose bond of friendship is thy choice

3. Sing praise to him the Lord of light! The Gods have made the God to be their messenger,

To bear oblation to the Gods.

4. Anger not him who is our guest! He is the bright God Agni, praised by many a man,

God Hotar, skilled in sacrifice.

5. May Agni, worshipped, bring us bliss: may the gift, blessed one! and sacrifice bring bliss.

Yea, may our eulogies bring bliss.

6. Thee have we chosen skilfullest in sacrifice, immortal Priest among the Gods,

Wise finisher of this holy rite.

7. Bring us that splendour, Agni, which may overcome each greedy fiend in our abode,

And the malicious wrath of men!

8. Soon as the eager Lord of men is friendly unto Manu's race

Agni averteth from us all the Rakshasas!

DECADE III Indra

1. Sing this, beside the flowing juice, to him your hero, much-invoked,

To please him as a mighty Bull

2. O Satakratu Indra, now rejoice with that carouse of thine

Which is most glorious of all!

3. Ye cows, protect the fount: the two mighty ones bless the sacrifice.

The handles twain are wrought of gold.

4. Sing praises that the horse may come; sing, Srutakaksha, that the cow

May come, that Indra's might may come

5. We make this Indra very strong to strike, the mighty Vritra dead:

A vigorous hero shall he be.

6. Based upon strength and victory and power, O Indra, is thy birth:

Thou, mighty one! art strong indeed,

7. The sacrifice made Indra great when he unrolled the earth, and made

Himself a diadem in heaven.

8. If I, O Indra, were, like thee, the single ruler over wealth

My worshipper should be rich in kine.

9. Pressers, blend Soma juice for him, each draught most excellent, for him

The brave, the hero, for his joy.

10. Here is the Soma juice expressed. O Vasu, drink till thou art full:

Undaunted God, we give it thee

DECADE IV Indra

1. Surya, thou mountest up to meet the hero famous for his wealth,

Who hurls the bolt and works for man.

2. Whatever, Vritra-slayer! thou, Surya hast risen upon to-day,

That, Indra, all is in thy power.

3. That Indra is our youthful friend, who with his trusty guidanceled

Turvasa, Yadu from afar.

4. O Indra, let not ill designs surround us in the sunbeams' light

This may we gain with thee for friend!

5. Indra, bring wealth that gives delight, the victor's ever-conquering wealth,

Most excellent, to be our aid

6. In mighty battle we invoke Indra, Indra is lesser fight,

The friend who bends his bolt at fiends.

7. In battle of a thousand arms Indra drank Kadru's Soma juice

There he displayed his manly might.

8. Faithful to thee, we sing aloud, heroic Indra, songs to thee

Mark, O good Lord, this act of ours!

9. Hitherward! they who light the flame and straightway trim the sacred grass,

Whose friend is Indra ever young.

10. Drive all our enemies away, smite down the foes who press around,

And bring the wealth for which we long!

DECADE V Indra and others

1. I Hear, as though 'twere close at hand, the cracking of the whips they hold:

They gather splendour on their way.

2. Indra, these friends of ours, supplied with Soma, wait and look to thee

As men with fodder to the herd.

3. Before his hot displeasure all the peoples, all the men bow down,

As rivers bow them to the sea.

4. We choose unto ourselves that high protection of the mighty Gods,

That it may help and succour us.

5. O Brahmanaspati, make thou Kakshivan Ausija a loud

Chanter of flowing Soma juice!

6. Much honoured with libations may the Vritra-slayer watch for us:

May Sakra listen to our prayer

7. Send us this day, God Savitar, prosperity with progeny

Drive thou the evil dream away!

8. Where is that ever-youthful Steer, strong-necked and never yet bent down?

What Brahman ministers to him?

9. There where the mountains downward slope, there at the meeting of the streams

The Sage was manifest by song.

10. Praise Indra whom our songs must laud, sole sovran of mankind, the chief

Most liberal who controlleth men

CHAPTER II

DECADE I Indra and others

1. Indra whose jaws are strong hath drunk of worshipping Sudaksha's draught,

The Soma juice with barley brew.

2. O Lord of ample wealth, these songs of praise have called aloud to thee,

Like milch-kine lowing to their calves!

3. Then straight they recognized the mystic name of the creative Steer,

There in the mansion of the Moon.

4. When Indra, strongest hero, brought the streams, the mighty waters down,

Pushan was standing by his side.

5. The Cow, the streaming mother of the liberal Maruts, pours her milk,

Harnessed to draw their chariots on.

6. Come, Lord of rapturous joys, to our libation with thy bay steeds, come

With bay steeds to the flowing juice

7. Presented strengthening gifts have sent Indra away at sacrifice,

With night, unto the cleansing bath.

8. I from my Father have received deep knowledge of eternal Law:

I was born like unto the Sun.

9. With Indra splendid feasts be ours, rich in all strengthening things, wherewith,

Wealthy in food, we may rejoice

10. Soma and Pushan, kind to him who travels to the Gods, provide

Dwellings all happy and secure.

DECADE II Indra

1. Invite ye Indra with a song to drink your draught of Soma steeds, juice,

All-conquering Satakratu, most munificent of all who live

2. Sing ye a song, to make him glad, to Indra, Lorc of tawny

The Soma-drinker, O my friends!

3. This, even this, O Indra, we implore: as thy devoted friends

The Kanvas praise thee with their hymns!

4. For Indra, lover of carouse, loud be our songs about the juice

Let poets sing the song of praise.

5. Here, Indra, is thy Soma draught, made pure upon the sacred grass:

Run hither, come and drink thereof

6. As a good cow to him who milks, we call the doer of good deeds

To our assistance duy by day.

7. Hero, the Soma being shed, I pour the juice for thee to drink

Sate thee and finish thy carouse!

8. The Soma, Indra, which is shed in saucers and in cups for thee,

Drink thou, for thou art lord thereof!

9. In every need, in every fray we call, as friends, to succour us,

Indra, the mightiest of all.

10. O come ye hither, sit ye down: to Indra sing ye forth your song,

Companions, bringing hymns of praise

DECADE III Indra

1. So, Lord of affluent gifts, this juice hath been expressed for thee with strength:

Drink of it, thou who lovest song!

2. Great is our Indra from of old; greatness be his, the Thunderer

Wide as the heaven extends his might.

3. Indra, as one with mighty arm, gather for us with thy right hand

Manifold and nutritious spoil!

4. Praise, even as he is known, with song Indra the guardian of the kine,

The Son of Truth, Lord of the brave.

5. With what help will he come to us, wonderful, ever-waxing friend?

With what most mighty company?

6. Thou speedest down to succour us this ever-conquering God of yours

Him who is drawn to all our songs.

7. To the assembly's wondrous Lord, the lovely friend of Indra, I

Had prayed for wisdom and successs.

8. May all thy paths beneath the sky whereby thou speddest Vyasva on,

Yea, let all spaces hear our voice

9. Bring to us all things excellent, O Satakratu, food and strength,

For, Indra, thou art kind to us!

10. Here is the Soma ready pressed: of this the Maruts, yea, of this,

Self-luminous the Asvins drink.

DECADE IV Indra and others

1. Tossing about, the active ones came nigh to Indra at his birth,

Winning themselves heroic might.

2. Never, O Gods, do we offend, nor are we ever obstinate

We walk as holy texts command.

3. Evening is come: sing loudly thou Atharvan's nobly singing son:

Give praise to Savitar the God!

4. Now Morning with her earliest light shines forth, dear daughter of the Sky:

High, Asvins, I extol your praise.

5. Armed with the bones of dead Dadhyach, Indra, with unresisted might

The nine-and-ninety Vritras slew.

6. Come, Indra, and delight thee with the juice at all our Soma feasts,

Protector, mighty in thy strength

7. O thou who slayest Vritras, come, O Indra, hither to our side,

Mighty one, with thy mighty aids!

8. That might of his shone brightly forth when Indra brought together, like

A skin, the worlds of heaven and earth,

9. This is thine own Thou drawest near, as turns a pigeon to his mate:

Thou carest, too, for this our prayer.

10. May Vata breathe his balm on us, healthful, delightful to our heart:

May he prolong our days of life

DECADE V Indra and others

1. Ne'er is he injured whom the Gods Varuna, Mitra, Aryam.

The excellently wise, protect.

2. According to our wish for kine, for steeds and chariots, as of old,

Be gracious to our wealthy chiefs

3. Indra, these spotted cows yield thee their butter and the milky draught,

Aiders, thereby, of sacrifice.

4. That thou much-lauded! many-named! mayst, with this thought, that longs for milk,

Come to each Soma sacrifice.

5. May bright Sarasvati, endowed with plenteous wealth and spoil, enriched

With prayer, desire the sacrifice.

6. Why 'mid the Nahusha tribes shall sate this Indra with his Soma juice?

He shall bring precious things to us.

7. Come, we have pressed the juice for thee; O Indra, drink this Soma here:

Sit thou on this my sacred grass

8. Great, unassailable must be the heavenly favour of the Three,

Varuna, Mitra, Aryaman.

9. We, Indra, Lord of ample wealth, our guide, depend on one like thee,

Thou driver of the tawny steeds!

BOOK III

CHAPTER I

DECADE I Indra

1. Let Soma juices make thee glad! Display thy bounty, Thunderer:

Drive off the enemies of prayer!

2. Drink our libation, Lord of hymns! with streams of meath thou art bedewed:

Yea, Indra, glory is thy gift.

3. Indra hath ever thought of you and tended you with care. The God,

Heroic Indra, is not checked.

4. Let the drops pass within thee as the rivers flow into the sea

O Indra, naught excelleth thee!

5. Indra, the singers with high praise, Indra reciters with their lauds,

Indra the choirs have glorified.

6. May Indra give, to aid us wealth handy that rules the skilful ones!

Yea, may the Strong give potent wealth

7. Verily Indra, conquering all, drives even mighty fear away,

For firm is he and swift to act.

8. These songs with every draught we pour come, lover of the song, to thee

As milch-kine hasten to their calves.

9. Indra and Wishan will we call for friendship and prosperity,

And for the winning of the spoil.

10. O Indra, Vritra-slayer, naught is better, mightier than thou

Verily there is none like thee!

DECADE II Indra

1. Him have I magnified, our Lord in common, guardian of your folk,

Discloser of great wealth in kine.

2. Songs have outpoured themselves to thee, Indra, the strong, the guardian Lord,

And with one will have risen to thee!

3. Good guidance hath the mortal man whom Arya-man, the Marut host,

And Mitras, void of guile, protect.

4. Bring us the wealth for which we long, O Indra, that which is concealed

In strong firm place precipitous.

5. Him your best Vritra-slayer, him the famous champion of mankind

I urge to great munificence.

6. Indra, may we adorn thy fame, fame of one like thee, hero! deck,

Sakra! thy fame at highest feast!

7. Indra, accept at break of day our Soma mixt with roasted corn,

With groats, with cake, with eulogies!

8. With waters' foam thou torest off, Indra, the head of Namuchi,

When thou o'ercamest all the foes.

9. Thine are these Soma juices, thine, Indra, those still to be expressed:

Enjoy them, Lord of princely wealth!

10. For thee, O Indra, Lord of light, Somas are pressed and grass is strewn:

Be gracious to thy worshippers!

1. We seeking strength, with Soma drops fill full your Indra like a well,

Most liberal, Lord of boundless might.

2. O Indra, even from that place come unto us with food that gives

A hundred, yea, a thousand powers!

3. The new-born Vritra-slayer asked his mother, as he seized his shaft,

Who are the, fierce and famous ones?

4. Let us call him to aid whose hands stretch far, the highly-lauded, who

Fulfils the work to favour us

5. Mitra who knoweth leadeth us, and Varuna who guideth straight,

And Aryaman in accord with Gods.

6. When, even as she were present here, red Dawn hath shone from far away,

She spreadeth light on every side.

7. Varuna, Mitra, sapient pair, pour fatness on our pastures, pour

Meath on the regions of the air!

8. And, at our sacrifices, these, sons, singers, have enlarged their bounds,

So that the cows must walk knee-deep.

9. Through all this world strode Vishnu: thrice his foot he planted, and the whole

Was gathered in his footstep's dust.

DECADE IV Indra

1. Pass by the wrathful offerer; speed the man who pours libation, drink

The juice which he presents to thee!

2. What is the word addressed to him, God great and excellently wise?

For this is what exalteth him.

3, His wealth who hath no store of kine hath ne'er found out recited laud,

Nor song of praises that is sung.

4. Lord of each thing that giveth strength, Indra delighteth most in lauds,

Borne by bay steeds, libations' friend.

5. With wealth to our libation come, be not thou angry with us, like

A great man with a youthful bride.

6. When, Vasu, wilt thou love the laud? Now let the Channel bring the stream.

The juice is ready to ferment.

7. After the Seasons. Indra, drink the Soma from the Brahman's gift:

Thy friendship is invincible!

S. O Indra, lover of the song, we are the singers of thy praise

O Soma-drinker, quicken us!

9. O Indra, in each fight and fray give to our bodies manly strength:

Strong Lord, grant ever-conquering might!

10. For so thou art the brave man's friend; a hero, too, art thou, and strong:

So may thine heart be won to us!

DECADE V Indra

1. Like kine unmilked we call aloud, hero, to thee, and sing thy praise,

Looker on heavenly light, Lord of this moving world, Lord, Indra, of what moveth not!

2. That we may win us wealth and power we poets, verily, call on thee:

In war men call on thee, Indra, the hero's Lord, in the steed's race-course call on thee:

3. To you will I sing Indra's praise who gives good gifts as well we know;

The praise of Maghavan who, rich in treasure, aids his singers with wealth thousandfold.

4. As cows low to their calves in stalls, so with our songs we glorify

This Indra, even your wondrous God who checks attack, who takes delight in precious juice.

5. Loud singing at the sacred rite where Soma flows we priests invoke

With haste, that he may help, as the bard's cherisher, Indra who findeth wealth for you

6. With Plenty for his true ally the active man will gain the spoil.

Your Indra, much-invoked, I bend with song, as bends a wright his wheel of solid wood.

7. Drink, Indra, of the savoury juice, and cheer thee with our milky draught!

Be, for our weal, our friend and sharer of the feast, and let thy wisdom guard us well!

8. For thou--come to the worshipper!--wilt find great wealth to make us rich.

Fill thyself full, O Maghavan, for gain of kine, full, Indra, for the gain of steeds!

9. Vasishtha will not overlook the lowliest one among you all

Beside our Soma juice effused to-day let all the Maruts drink with eager haste!

10. Glorify naught besides, O friends; so shall no sorrow trouble you!

Praise only mighty Indra when the juice is shed, and say your lauds repeatedly!

CHAPTER II

DECADE I Indra

1. No one by deed attains to him who works and strengthens evermore:

No, not by sacrifice, to Indra. praised of all, resistless, daring, bold in might.

2 He without ligature, before making incision in the neck,

Closed up the wound again, most wealthy Maghavan, who healeth the dissevered parts.

3. A thousand and a hundred steeds are harnessed to thy golden car:

Yoked by devotion, Indra, let the long-maned bays bring thee to drink the Soma juice!

4. Come hither, Indra, with bay steeds, joyous, with tails like peacock's plumes!

Let no men check thy course as fowlers stay the bird: pass o'er them as o'er desert lands!

5. Thou as a God, O mightiest, verily blessest mortal man.

O Maghavan, there is no comforter but thou: Indra, I speak my words to thee.

6. O Indra, thou art far-renowned, impetuous Lord of power and might.

Alone, the never-conquered guardian of mankind, thou smitest

down resistless foes.

7. Indra for worship of the Gods, Indra while sacrifice proceeds,

Indra, as warriors in the battle-shock, we call, Indra that we may win the spoil.

8. May these my songs of praise exalt thee, Lord, who hast abundant wealth!

Men skilled in holy hymns, pure, with the hues of fire, have sung them with their lauds to thee.

9. These songs of ours exceeding sweet, these hymns of praise ascend to thee,

Like ever-conquering chariots that display their strength gain wealth and give unfailing help.

10. Even as the wild-bull, when he thirsts, goes to the desert's watery pool,

Come to us quickly both at morning and at eve, and with the Kanvas drink thy fill!

DECADE II Indra and others

1. Indra, with all thy saving helps assist us, Lord of power and might!

For after thee we follow even as glorious bliss, thee, hero, finderout of wealth.

2. O Indra, Lord of light, what joys thou broughtest from the Asuras,

Prosper therewith, O Maghavan, him who lauds that deed, and those whose grass is trimmed for thee!

3. To Aryaman and Mitra sing a reverent song, O pious one,

A pleasant hymn to Varuna who shelters us: sing ye a laud unto the Kings!

4. Men with their lauds are urging thee, Indra, to drink the Soma first.

The Ribhus in accord have lifted up their voice, and Rudras sung thee as the first.

5. Sing to your lofty Indra, sing, Maruts, a holy hymn of praise

Let Satakratu, Vritra-slayer, slay the foe with hundred-knotted thunderbolt!

6. To Indra sing the lofty hymn, Maruts! that slays the Vritras best,

Whereby the holy ones created for the God the light divine that ever wakes.

7. O Indra, give us wisdom as a sire gives wisdom to his sons

Guide us, O much-invoked, in this our way: may we still live and look upon the light!

8. O Indra, turn us not away: be present with us at our feast

For thou art our protection, yea, thou art our kin: O Indra, turn us not away!

9. We compass these like waters, we whose grass is trimmed and Soma pressed.

Here where the filter pours its stream, thy worshippers round

thee, O Vritra-slayer, sit.

10. All strength and valour that is found, Indra, in tribes of Nahushas,

And all the splendid fame that the Five Tribes enjoy, bring, yea, all manly powers at once!

DECADE III Indra

1. Yea, verily thou art a Bull, our guardian, rushing like a bull:

Thou, mighty one, art celebrated as a Bull, famed as a Bull both near and far.

2. Whether, O Sakra, thou be far, or, Vritra-slayer, near at hand,

Thence by heaven-reaching songs he who bath pressed the juice invites thee with thy long-maned steeds.

3. In the wild raptures of the juice sing to your hero with high laud, to him the wise,

To Indra glorious in his name, the mighty one, even as the hymn alloweth it!

4. O Indra, give us for our weal a triple refuge, triply strong!

Bestow a dwelling-place on our rich lords and me, and keep thy dart afar from these!

5. Turning, as 'twere, to meet the Sun enjoy from Indra all good things!

When he who will be born is born with power we look to treasures as our heritage.

6. The godless mortal gaineth not this food, O thou whose life is long!

But one who yokes the bright-hued horses, Etasas; then Indra yokes his tawny steeds.

7. Draw near unto our Indra who must be invoked in every fight!

Come, thou most mighty Vritra-slayer, meet for praise, come to, libations and to hymns!

8. Thine, Indra, is the lowest wealth, thou cherishest the midmost wealth,

Thou ever rulest all the highest: in the fray for cattle none resisteth thee.

9. Where art thou? Whither art thou gone? For many a place attracts thy mind.

Haste, warrior, fort-destroyer, Lord of battle's din! haste, holy songs have sounded forth!

10. Here, verily, yesterday we let the thunder-wielder drink his fill.

Bring him the juice poured forth in sacrifice to-day. Now range you by the glorious one!

DECADE IV Indra

1. He who as sovran Lord of men moves with his chariots unrestrained,

The Vritra-slayer, vanquisher of fighting hosts, pre-eminent, is praised in song.

2. Indra, give us security from that whereof we are afraid

Help us, O Maghavan, let thy favour aid us thus; drive away foes and enemies!

3. Strong pillar thou, Lord of the home! armour of Soma-offerers!

The drop of Soma breaketh all the strongholds down, and Indra is the Rishis' friend.

4. Verily, Surya, thou art great; truly, Aditya, thou art great!

O most admired for greatness of thy majesty, God, by thy greatness thou art great!

5. Indra! thy friend, when fair of form and rich in chariots, steeds, and kine,

Hath ever vital power that gives him strength, and joins the company with radiant men.

6. O Indra, if a hundred heavens and if a hundred earths were thine,--

No, not a hundred suns could match thee at thy birth, not both the worlds, O Thunderer!

7. Though, Indra, thou art called by men eastward and west ward, north and south,

Thou chiefly art with Anava and Turvasa, brave champion urged by men to come.

8. Indra whose wealth is in thyself, what mortal will attack this man?

The strong will win the spoil on the decisive day through faith in thee, O Maghavan!

9. First, Indra! Agni! hath this Maid come footless unto those with feet.

Stretching her head and speaking loudly with her tongue, she hath gone downward thirty steps.

10. Come, Indra, very near to us with aids of firmly-based resolve

Come, most auspicious, with thy most auspicious help; good kinsman, with good kinsmen come!

DECADE V Indra.

1. Call to your aid the eternal one who shoots and none may shoot at him,

Inciter, swift, victorious, best of charioteers, unconquered, Tugriya's strengthener!

2. Let none, no, not thy worshippers, delay thee far away from us

Even from faraway come thou unto our feast, or listen if' already here!

3. For Indra Soma-drinker, armed with thunder, press the Soma juice;

Make ready your dressed meats: cause him to favour us! The giver blesses him who gives.

4. We call upon that Indra who, most active, ever slays the foe

With boundless spirit, Lord of heroes, manliest one, help thou and prosper us in fight!

5. Ye rich in strength, through your great power vouchsafe us blessings day and night!

The offerings which we bring to you shall never fail gifts brought by us shall never fail.

6. Whenever mortal worshipper will sing a bounteous giver's praise,

Let him with song inspired laud Varuna who supports the folk who follow varied rites.

7. Drink milk to Indra in the joy of Soma juice, Medhyatithi!

To golden Indra ever close to his bay steeds, the thunder-armed, the golden one!

8. Both boons,-may Indra, hitherward turned listen to this prayer of ours,

And mightiest Maghavar, with thought inclined to us come near to drink the Soma juice!

9. Not for an ample price dost thou, Stone-caster! give thyself away,

Not for a thousand, Thunderer! nor ten thousand, nor a hundred. Lord of countless wealth!

10. O Indra, thou art more to me than sire or niggard brother is.

Thou and my mother, O good Lord, appear alike, to give me wealth abundantly.

BOOK IV

CHAPTER I

DECADE I Indra and others

1. These Soma juice mixt with curd have been expressed for Indra here:

Come with thy bay steeds, Thunder-wielder, to our home, to drink them till they make thee glad!

2. Indra, these Somas with their lauds have been prepared for thy delight.

Drink of the pleasant juice and listen to our songs; lover of song, reward the hymn!

3. I call on thee, Sabardugha, this day, inspirer of the psalm.

Indra, the richly-yielding milch-cow who provides unfailing food in ample stream.

4. Indra, the strong and lofty hills are powerless to bar thy way

None stays that act of thine when thou wouldst fain give wealth to one like me who sings thy praise.

5. Who knows what vital power he wins, drinking beside the flowing juice?

This is the fair-cheeked. God who, joying in the draught, breaks down the castles in his strength.

6. What time thou castest from his seat and punishest the riteless man,

Strengthen for opulence, O Indra Maghavan, our plant desired by many a one!

7. Let Tvashtar, Brahmanaspati, Parjanya guard our heavenly word.

Aditi with her sons, the brothers, guard for us the invincible, the saving word!

8. Ne'er art thou fruitless, Indra, ne'er dost thou desert the worshipper:

But now, O Maghavan, thy bounty as a God is poured forth ever more and more.

9. Best slayer of the Vritras, yoke thy bay steeds, Indra, far away

Come with the high ones hither, Maghavan, to us, mighty, to, drink the Soma juice!

10. O Thunderer, zealous worshippers gave thee drink this time yesterday:

So, Indra, listen here to him who offers lauds: come near unto, our dwelling-place!

DECADE II

1. Advancing, sending forth her rays, the daughter of the Sky is seen.

The mighty one lays bare the darkness with her eye, the friendly Lady makes the light.

2. These morning sacrifices call you, Asvins, at the break of day.

For help have I invoked you rich in power and might: for, house by house, ye visit all.

3. Where are ye, Gods? What mortal man, O Asvins, glows with zeal for you,

Urging you with the crushing stone and with the stalk of Soma thus or otherwise?

4. This sweetest Soma juice hath been expressed for you at morning rites.

Asvins, drink this prepared ere yesterday and give treasures to him who offers it!

5. Let me not, still beseeching thee with might and sound of Soma drops,

Anger at sacrifice a fierce wild creature! Who would not beseech the almighty one!

6. Adhvaryu, let the Soma flow, for Indra longs to drink thereof.

He even now hath yoked his vigorous bay steeds: the Vritraslayer hath come nigh.

7. Bring thou all this unto the good, O Indra, to the old and young!

For, Maghavan, thou art rich in treasures from of old, to be invoked in every fight.

8. If I, O Indra, were the lord of riches ample as thine own,

I would support the singer, God who scatterest wealth! and not abandon him to woe.

9. Thou in thy battles, Indra, art subduer of all hostile bands.

Father art thou, all-conquering, cancelling the curse, thou victor of the vanquisher!

10. For in thy might thou stretchest out beyond the mansions of the sky.

The earthly region, Indra, comprehends thee not. Thou hast waxed mighty over all.

DECADE III

1. Pressed is the juice divine with milk commingled: thereto hath Indra ever been accustomed.

We wake thee, Lord of bays, with sacrifices: mark this our laud in the wild joys of Soma!

2. A home is made for thee to dwell in, Indra: O much-invoked one, with the men go thither!

Thou, that thou mayest guard us and increase us, givest us wealth and joyest in the Somas.

3. The well thou clavest, settest free the fountains, and gavest rest to floods that were obstructed.

Thou, Indra, laying the great mountain open, slaying the Ddnava, didst loose the torrents.

4. When we have pressed the juice we laud thee, Indra, most valorous! even about to win the booty.

Bring us prosperity, and by thy great wisdom, under thine own protection, may we conquer!

5. Thy right hand have we grasped in ours, O Indra, longing, thou very Lord of wealth, for treasures.

Because we know thee, hero, Lord of cattle: vouchsafe us mighty and resplendent riches!

6. Men call on Indra in the armed encounter that he may make the hymns they sing decisive.

Hero in combat and in love of glory, give us a portion of the stall of cattle!

7. Like birds of beauteous wing the Priyamedhas, Rishis, imploring, have come nigh to Indra.

Dispel the darkness and fill full our vision: deliver us as men whom snares entangle!

8. They gaze on thee with longing in their spirit, as on a strongwinged bird that mounteth sky-ward;

On thee with wings of gold, Varuna's envoy, the Bird that hasteneth to the home of Yama.

9. First in the ancient time was Prayer engendered: Vena disclosed the bright ones from the summit,

Laid bare this world's lowest and highest regions, womb of the existent and the non-existent.

10. They have prepared and fashioned for this hero words never matched, most plentiful, most auspicious,

For him the ancient, great, strong, energetic, the very mighty wielder of the thunder.

DECADE IV Indra

1. The black drop sank in Ansumati's bosom, advancing with ten thousand round about it.

Indra with might longed for it as it panted: the hero-hearted King laid down his weapons.

2. Flying in terror from the snort of Vritra all deities who were thy friends forsook thee.

So, Indra, with the Maruts be thy friendship: in all these battles thou shalt be the victor.

3. The old hath waked the young Moon from his slumber who runs his circling course with many round him.

Behold the God's high wisdom in its greatness: he who died yesterday to-day is living.

4. Then, at thy birth, thou wast the foeman, Indra, of those the seven who ne'er had met a rival.

The hidden pair, heaven and the earth, thou foundest, and to the mighty worlds thou gavest pleasure.

5. A friend we count thee, sharp-edged, thunder-wielder, Steer strong of body, overthrowing many.

Thou, helping, causest pious tribes to conquer: Indra, I laud the, heavenly Vritra-slayer.

6. Bring to the wise, the great, who waxeth mighty your offerings,. and make ready your devotion!

Go forth to many tribes as man's controller!

7. Call we on Maghavan, auspicious Indra, best hero in this fight where spoil is gathered,

Strong, listening to give us aid in battles, who slays the Vritras, wins and gathers riches!

8. Prayers have been offered up-through love of glory: Vasishtha, honour Indra in the battle!

He who with fame extends through all existence hears words which I, his faithful servant, utter.

9. May the sweet Soma juices make him happy to cast his quoit that lies in depth of waters!

Thou from the udder which o'er earth is fastened hast poured the milk into the kine and herbage.

DECADE V Indra and others

1. This vigorous one whom deities commission, the conqueror of cars, the strong and mighty,

Swift, fleet to battle, with uninjured fellies, even Tarkshya for our weal will we call hither.

2. Indra the rescuer, Indra the helper, hero who listens at each invocation,

Sakra I call, Indra invoked of many. May Indra Maghavan accept our presents!

3. Indra whose right hand wields the bolt we worship, driver of bay steeds seeking sundered courses.

Shaking his beard with might he hath arisen, terrible with his weapons, with his bounty.

4. The ever-slaying, bold and furious Indra, the bright bolt's Lord, the strong, the great, the boundless,

Who slayeth Vritra and acquireth booty, giver of blessings, Maghavan the bounteous.

5. The man who lies in wait and fights against us, deeming himself a giant or a hero,--

By battle or with strength destroy him, Indra! With thy help, manly-souled! may we be victors!

6. He whom men call when striving with their foemen, or speeding onward in

array of battle,

Whom bards incite where heroes win the booty, or in the way to waters, He is Indra.

7. On a high car, O Parvata and Indra, bring pleasant viands, with brave heroes, hither!

Enjoy our presents, Gods, at sacrifices: wax strong by hymns, rejoice in our oblation!

8. In ceaseless flow hath he poured forth his praises, as waters from the ocean's depth, to Indra,

Who to his car on both its sides securely hath fixed the earth and heaven as with an axle.

9. May our friends turn thee hitherward to friendship! Mayst thou approach us even o'er many rivers!

May the Disposer, radiant in this mansion with special lustre, bring the father's offspring!

10. Who yokes to-day unto the pole of Order the strong and passionate steers of checkless spirit,

Health-bringing, bearing in their mouths no fodder? Long shall he live who richly pays their service.

CHAPTER II

DECADE I Indra

1. The singers hymn thee, they who chant the psalm of praise are lauding thee.

The Brahmans have exalted thee, O Satakratu, like a pole.

2. All sacred-songs have magnified Indra expansive as the sea,

Best of all warriors borne on cars, the Lord of heroes, Lord of strength.

3. This poured libation, Indra, drink, immortal, gladdening, excellent:

Streams of the bright have flowed to thee here at the seat of holy Law.

4. Stone-darting Indra, wondrous God, what wealth thou hast not given me here,

That bounty, treasure-finder! bring, filling full both thy hands, to us!

5. O Indra, hear Tiraschi's call, the call of him who serveth thee!

Satisfy him with wealth of kine and valiant offspring! Great art thou.

6. This Soma hath been pressed for thee, O Indra: bold one, mightiest, come!

May Indra-vigour fill thee full, as Surya fills mid-air with rays

7. Come hither, Indra, with thy bays, come thou to Kanva's eulogy!

Ye by command of yonder Dyaus, God bright by day! have gone to heaven.

8. Song-lover! like a charioteer come songs to thee when Soma flows.

Together, they have called to thee as mother-kine unto their calves.

9. Come now and let us glorify pure Indra with pure Sama hymn!

Let milk-blent juice delight him made stronger with pure, pure songs of praise!

10. That which, most wealthy, makes you rich, in splendours most illustrious,

Soma is pressed: thy gladdening drink, Indra libation's Lord! is this.

DECADE II Indra. Dadhikravan

1. Bring forth oblations to the God who knoweth all who fain would drink,

The wanderer, lagging not behind the hero, coming nigh with speed!

2. To us the mighty, lying in all vital power, who resteth in the deep, who standeth in the east.

Drive thou the awful word away.

3. Even as a car to give us aid, we draw thee nigh to favour us,

Strong in thy deeds, quelling attack, Indra, Lord, mightiest! of the brave.

4. With powers of mighty ones hath he, the friend, the ancient, been equipped,

Through whom our father Manu made prayers efficacious with the Gods.

5. What time the swift and shining steeds, yoked to the chariots, draw them on,

Drinking the sweet delightful juice, there men perform their glorious acts.

6. Him for your sake I glorify as Lord of Strength who wrongeth none,

Indra the hero, mightiest, all-conquering and omniscient.

7. I with my praise have glorified strong Dadhikravan, conquering steed

Sweet may he make our mouths: may he prolong the days we have to live!

8. Render of forts, the young, the wise, of strength unmeasured, was he born,

Sustainer of each sacred rite, Indra, the Thunderer, much-extolled.

DECADE III Indra and others

1. Offer the triple sacred draught to Indu hero-worshipper!

With hymn and plenty he invites you to complete the sacrifice.

2. Those whom they call the attendant pair of Kasyapa who knows the light,

Lords of each holy duty when the wise have honoured sacrifice.

3. Sing, sing ye forth your songs of praise, men, Priya-medhas, sing your songs:

Yea, let young children sing their lauds: yea, glorify our firm stronghold!

4. To Indra must a laud be said, a joy to him who freely gives,

That Sakra may be joyful in our friendship and the juice we pour.

5. Your Lord of might that ne'er hath bent, that ruleth over all mankind,

I call, that he, as he is wont, may aid the chariots and the men.

6. Even he who is thine own, through thought of Heaven, of mortal man who toils,

He with the help of lofty Dyaus comes safe through straits of enmity.

7. Wide, Indra Satakratu, spreads the bounty of thine ample grace:

So, good and liberal giver, known to all men, send us splendid wealth!

8. Bright Ushas, when thy times return, all quadrupeds and bipeds stir,

And round about flock winged birds from all the boundaries of heaven.

9. Ye Gods who yonder have your home amid the luminous realm of heaven,

What count ye right? what endless life? What is the ancient call on you?

10. We offer laud and psalm wherewith men celebrate their holy rites.

They govern at the sacred place and bear the sacrifice to Gods.

DECADE IV Indra

1. Heroes of one accord brought forth and formed for kingship Indra who wins the victory in all encounters,

For power, in firmness, in the field, the great destroyer, fierce and exceeding strong,rstalwart and full of vigour.

2. I trust in thy first wrathful deed, O Indra, when thou slewest Vritra and didst work to profit man;

When the two world-halves fled for refuge unto thee, and earth even trembled at thy strength, O Thunder-armed!

3. Come all with might together to the Lord of heaven, the only one who is indeed the guestof men.

He is the first: to him who fain would come to us all pathways turn; he is in truth the only one.

4. Thine, Indra, praised of many, excellently rich, are we who trusting in thy help draw near to thee.

For none but thou, song-lover, shall receive our lauds: as Earth loves all her creatures, welcome this our hymn!

5. High hymns have sounded forth the praise of Maghavan, supporter of mankind, of Indra meet for lauds;

Him who hath waxen mighty, much-invoked with prayers, immortal one whose praise each day is sung aloud.

6. In perfect unison have all your longing hymns that find the light of heaven sounded forth Indra's praise.

As wives embrace their lord, the comely bridegroom, so they compass Maghavan about that he may help.

7. Make glad with songs that Ram whom many men invoke, worthy hymns of praise, Indra the sea of wealth;

Whose boons spread like the heavens, the - lover of mankind: sing praise to him the Sage, most liberal for our good!

8. I glorify that Ram who finds the light of heaven, whose hundred strong and mighty ones go forth with him.

With prayers may I turn hither Indra to mine aid;-the car which like a swift steed hasteth to the call!

9. Filled full of fatness, compassing all things that be, wide, spacious, dropping meath, beautiful in their form,

The heaven and the earth by Varuna's decree, unwasting, rich in germs, stand parted each from each.

10. As like the Morning, thou hast filled, O Indra, both the earth. and heaven,

So as the mighty one, great King of all the mighty race of men, the Goddess mother brought thee forth, the blessed mother gave thee life.

11. Sing, with oblation, praise to him who maketh glad, who with. Rijisvan drove the dusky brood away!

Let us, desiring help, call him for friendship, him the strong, the Marut-girt, whose right hand wields the bolt!

DECADE V Indra

I. When Somas flow thou makest pure, Indra, thy mind that merits laud

For gain of strength that ever grows: for great is he.

2. Sing forth to him whom many men invoke, to him whom many laud:

Invite the potent Indra with your songs of praise

3. We sing this strong and wild delight of thine which conquer; in the fray,

Which, Caster of the Stone! gives room and shines like gold,

4. Whether thou drink the Soma by Vishnu's or Trita Aptya's side,

Or with the Maruts, Indra! quaff the following drops.

5. Come, priest, and of the savoury juice pour forth a yet more gladdening draught:

So is the hero praised who ever prospers us.

6. Pour out the drops for Indra; let him drink the meath of Soma juice!

He through his majesty sends forth his bounteous gifts.

7. Come, sing we praise to Indra, friends! the hero who deserves the laud,

Him who with none to aid o'ercomes all tribes of men.

8. Sing ye a psalm to Indra, sing a great song to the lofty Sage,

To him who maketh prayer, inspired who loveth laud!

9. He who alone bestoweth wealth on mortal man who offereth gifts

Is Indra only, potent Lord whom none resist.

10. Companions, let us learn a prayer to Indra, to the Thunderer,

To glorify your bold and most heroic friend!

PART SECOND

BOOK I
CHAPTER I

Om. Glory to the Samaveda! to Lord Ganesa glory! Om.

I Soma Pavamana

1. Sing forth to Indu, O ye men, to him who now is purified,

Fain to pay worship to the Gods!

2, Together with thy pleasant juice the Atharvans have commingled. milk.

Divine, God-loving, for the God.

3. Bring health to cattle with thy flow, health to the people, health, tc steeds,

Health, O thou King, to growing plants!

II Soma Pavamana

1. Bright are these Somas blent with milk, with light that flashes brilliantly,

And form that shouteth all around.

2. Roused by his drivers and sent forth, the strong Steed hath come: nigh for spoil,

As warriors when they stand arrayed.

3. Specially, Soma, Sage, by day, coming together for our weal,

Like Surya, flow for us to see!

III Soma Pavamana

1. The streams of Pavamana, thine, Sage, mighty one, have poured them forth,

Like coursers eager for renown.

2. They have been poured upon the Reece towards the meath-distilling vat:

The holy songs have rung aloud.

3. Like milch-kine coming home, the drops of Soma juice have reached the lake,

Have reached the shrine of sacrifice

IV Agni

1. Come, Agni, praised with song to feast and sacrificial offerings: sit

As Hotar on the holy grass!

2. So, Angiras, we make thee strong with fuel and with holy oil.

Blaze high, thou youngest of the Gods!

3. For us thou winnest, Agni, God, heroic strength exceeding great, Far-spreading and of high renown.

V Mitra Varuna

1. Varuna, Mitra, sapient pair, pour fatness on our pastures, pour

Meath on the regions of the air!

2, Gladdened by homage, ruling far, ye reign by majesty of might,

Pure in your ways, for evermore.

3. Lauded by Jamadagni's song, sit in the shrine of sacrifice:

Drink Soma, ye who strengthen Law!

VI Indra

1. Come, we have pressed theJuice for thee; O Indra, drink this Soma here:
Sit thou on this my sacred grass!
2. O Indra, let thy long-maned bays, yoked by prayer, bring thee hitherward!
Give ear and listen to our prayers!
3. We Soma-bearing Brahmans call thee Soma-drinker with thy friend,
We, Indra, bringing Soma juice.

VII Indra Agni

1. Indra and Agni, moved by songs, come to the juice, the precious dew:
Drink ye thereof, impelled by prayer!
2. Indra and Agni, with the man who lauds comes visible sacrifice:
So drink ye both this flowing juice!
3. With force of sacrifice I seek Indra, Agni who love the wise:
With Soma let them sate them here!

VIII Soma Pavamana

1. High is thy juice's birth: though set in heaven, on earth it hath obtained
Dread sheltering power and great renown.
2. Finder of room and freedom, flow for Indra whom we must adore,
For Varuna and the Marut host!
3. Striving to win, with him we gain all riches from the enemy,
Yea, all the glories of mankind,

IX Soma Pavamana

1. Cleansing thee, Soma, in thy stream, thou flowest in watery robe.

Giver of wealth, thou sittest in the place of Law, O God, a fountain made of gold.

2. He, milking for dear meath the heavenly udder, hath sat in the ancient gathering-place.

Washed by the men, far-sighted, strong, thou streamest to ther honourable reservoir.

X Soma Pavamana

1. Run onward to the reservoir and seat thee: cleansed by the men speed forward to the battle.

Making thee glossy like an able courser, forth to the sacred grass with reins they lead thee.

2. Indu, the well-armed God is flowing onward, he who averts the curse and guards the homesteads.

Father, begetter of the Gods, most skilful, the buttress of the heavens and earth's supporter.

XI Indra

1. Like kine unmilked we call aloud, hero, to thee, and sing thy

praise,

Looker on heavenly light, Lord of this moving world, Lord, Indra! of what moveth not.

2. None other like to thee, of earth or of the heavens, hath been or ever will be born.

Desiring horses, Indra Maghavan! and kine, as men of might we call on thee.

XII Indra

1. With what help will he come to us, wonderful, everwaxing friend?

With what most mighty company?

2. What genuine and most liberal draught will spirit thee with juice to burst

Open e'en strongly-guarded wealth?

3. Do thou who art protector of us thy friends who praise thee

With hundred aids approach us!

XIII Indra

1. As cows low to their calves in stalls, so with our songs we glorify

This Indra, even your wondrous God who checks attack, who takes delight in precious juice.

2. Celestial, bounteous giver, girt about with might, rich, mountain-like, in pleasant things,--

Him swift we seek for foodful booty rich in kine, brought hundredfold and thousandfold.

XIV Indra

1. Loud-singing at tbe sacred rite where Soma flows, we priests invoke.

With haste, that he may help, as the bard's cherisher. Indra who findeth wealth for you.

2. Whom, fair of cheek, in rapture of the juice, the firm resistless slayers hinder not:

Giver of glorious wealth to him who sings his praise, honouring him who toils and pours.

XV Soma Pavamana

1. In sweetest and most gladdening stream flow pure, O Soma, on thy way,

Pressed out for Indra, for his drink!

2. Fiend-queller, friend of all men, he hath reached his shrine, his dwelling-place.

Within the iron-hammered vat.

3. Be thou best Vritra-slayer, best granter of room, most liberal:

Promote our wealthy princes' gifts!

XVI Soma Pavamana

1. For Indra flow, thou Soma, on, as most inspiring drink, most rich in sweets,

Great, most Celestial, gladdening drink!

2. Thou of whom having drunk the Steer acts like a steer: having drunk this that finds the light,

He, excellently wise, hath come anear to food and booty, even as Etasa.

XVII Indra

1. To Indra, to the mighty let these golden-coloured juices go,

Drops born as Law prescribes, that find the light of heaven!

2. This juice that gathers spoil flows, pressed, for Indra, for his maintenance.

Soma bethinks him of the conqueror, as he knows.

3. Yea, Indra in the joys of this obtains the grasp that gathers spoil,

And, winning waters, wields the mighty thunderbolt.

XVIII Soma Pavamana.

1. For first possession of your juice, for the exhilarating drink,

Drive ye away the dog, my friends, drive ye the long-tongued dog away!

2. He who with purifying stream, effused, comes flowing hitherward,

Indu, is like an able steed.

3. With prayer all-reaching let the men tend unassailable Soma: be-

The stones prepared for sacrifice!

XIX Soma Pavamana

1. Graciously- minded he is flowing on his way to win cear names o'er which the youthful one grows great.

The mighty and far-seeing one hath mounted now the mighty

Surya's car which moves to every side.

2. The speaker, unassailable master of this prayer, the tongue of sacrifice, pours forth the pleasant meath.

As son be sets the name of mother and of sire in the far distance, in the third bright realm of heaven.

3. Sending forth flashes he hath bellowed to the jars, led by the men into the golden reservoir.

The milkers of the sacrifice have sung to him: Lord of three heights, thou shinest brightly o'er the Dawns.

XX Agni

1. Sing to your Agni with each song, at every sacrifice for strength!

Come, let us praise the wise and everlasting God, even as a well-beloved friend:

2. The Son of Strength; for is be not our gracious Lcrd? Let us serve him who bears our gifts!

In battles may he be our help and strengthener, yea, be the saviour of our lives!

XXI Agni

1. O Agni, come; far other songs of praise will I sing forth to thee.

Wax mighty with these Soma drops!

2. Where'er thy mind applies itself, vigour preeminent hast thou:

There wilt thou gain a dwelling-place.

3. Not for a moment only lasts thy bounty, Lord of many men:

Our service therefore shalt thou gain.

XXII Indra

1. We call on thee, O matchless one. We, seeking help, possessing nothing firm ourselves.

Call on thee, wondrous, thunder-armed:

2. On thee for aid in sacrifice, This youth of ours, the bold, the terrible, bath gone forth.

We therefore, we thy friends, Indra, have chosen thee, spoil winner, as our succourer.

XXIII Indra

1. So, Indra, friend of song, do we draw near to thee with longing; we have streamed to thee

Coming like floods that follow floods.

2. As rivers swell the ocean, so, hero, our prayers increase thy might,

Though of thyself, O Thunderer, waxing day by day.

3. With holy song they bind to the broad wide-yoked car the bay steeds of the quickening God,

Bearers of Indra, yoked by word.

CHAPTER II

I Indra

I. Invite ye Indra with a song to drink your draught cf Soma juicel

All-conquering Satakratu, most munificent of all who live!

2. Lauded by many, much-invoked, leader of song renowned of old:

His name is Indra, tell it forth!

3. Indra, the dancer, be to us the giver of abundant wealth:

The mighty bring it us knee-deep!

II Indra

1. Sing ye a song, to make him glad, to Indra, Lord of tawny steeds,

The Soma-drinker, O my friends!

2. To him, the bounteous, say the laud, and let us glorify, as men

May do, the giver of true gifts!

3. O Indra, Lord of boundless might, for us thou seekest spoil and kine,

Thou seekest gold for us, good Lord!

III Indra

1. This, even this, O Indra, we implore: as thy devoted friends,

The Kanvas praise thee with their hymns.

2. Naught else, O Thunderer, have I praised in the skilled singer's eulogy;

On thy laud only have I thought.

3. The Gods seek him who presses out the Soma; they desire not sleep:

They punish sloth unweariedly

IV Indra

1. For Indra, lover of carouse, loud be our songs about the juice:

Let poets sing the song of praise

2. We summon Indra to the draught, in whom all glories rest, in whom

The seven communities rejoice.

3. At the Trikadrukas the Gods span sacrifice that stirs the mind:

Let our songs aid and prosper it!

V Indra

1. Here, Indra, is thy Soma draught, made pure upon the sacred grass:

Run hither, come and drink thereof!

2. Strong-rayed! adored with earnest hymns! this juice is shed for thy delight:

Thou art invoked, Akhandala!

3. To Kundapayya, grandson's son, grandson of Sringavrish! to thee,

To him have I addressed my thought.

VI Indra

1. Indra, as one with mighty arm, gather for us with thy right hand,

Manifold and nutritious spoil!

2. We know thee mighty in thy deeds, of mighty bounty, mighty wealth.

Mighty in measure, prompt to aid.

3. Hero when thou wouldst give thy gifts, neither the Gods nor mortal men

Restrain thee like a fearful bull.

VII Indra

1. Hero, the Soma being shed, I pour the juice for thee to drink:

Sate thee and finish thy carouse!

2. Let not the fools, or those who mock, beguile thee when they seek thine aid:

Love not the enemy of prayer!

3. Here let them cheer thee well supplied with milk to great munificence:

Drink as the wild bull drinks the lake!

VIII Indra

I. Here is the Soma juice expressed: O Vasu, drink till thou art full!

Undaunted God, we give it thee!

2. Washed by the men, pressed out with stones, strained through the filter made of wool,

'Tis like a courser bathed in streams.

3. This juice have we made sweet for thee like barley, blending it with milk.

Indra, I call thee to our feast.

IX Indra

1. So, Lord of affluent gifts, this juice hath been expressed for thee with strength:

Drink of it, thou who lovest song!

2. Incline thy body to the juice which suits thy godlike nature well:

Thee, Soma-lover! let it cheer!

3. O Indra, let it enter both thy flanks, enter thy head with prayer,

With bounty, hero! both thine arms!

X Indra

1. O Come ye hither, sit ye down; to Indra sing ye forth your song,

Companions, bringing hymns of praise,

2. Laud Indra, richest of the rich, who ruleth over noblest wealth,

Beside the flowing Soma juice!

3. May he stand near us in our need with all abundance, for our wealth:

With strength may he come nigh to us!

XI Indra

1. In every need, in every fray we call, as friends to succour us,

Indra, the mightiest of all.

2. I call him, mighty to resist, the hero of our ancient home,

Thee whom my sire invoked of old.

3. If he will hear us, let him come with succour of a thousand kinds,

With strength and riches, to our call!

XI Indra

1. When Somas flow thou makest pure, Indra, thy mind that merits laud,

For gain of strength that ever grows: for great is he.

2. In heaven's first region, in the seat of Gods, is he who brings success,

Most glorious, prompt to save, who wins the waterfloods.

3. Him I invoke, to win the spoil, even mighty Indra for the fray.

Be thou most near to us for bliss, a friend to aid!

XIII Agni

1. With this mine homage I invoke Agni for you, the Son of Strength.

Dear, wisest envoy, skilled in noble sacrifice, immortal, messanger of all.

2. His two red horses, all-supporting, let him yoke: let him, well-worshipped, urge them fast!

Then hath the sacrifice good prayers and happy end, the heavenly gift of wealth to men.

XIV Dawn

1. Advancing, sending forth her rays, the daughter of the Sky is seen.

The mighty one lays bare the darkness with her eye, the friendly Lady makes the light.

2. The Sun ascending, the refulgent star, pours down his beams. together with the Dawn.

O Dawn, at thine arising, and, the Sun's, may we attain the share allotted us!

XV Asvins

1. These morning sacrifices call you, Asvins, at the break of day.

For help have I invoked you rich in power and might: for, house by house, ye visit all.

2. Ye, heroes, have bestowed wonderful nourishment: send it to him whose songs are sweet.

One-minded, both of you, drive your car down to us: drink yethe savoury Soma juice!

XVI Soma Pavamana.

1. After his ancient splendour, they, the bold, have drawn the bright milk from

The Sage who wins a thousand spoils.

2. In aspect he is like the Sun: he runneth forward to the lakes: Seven currents flowing to the sky.

3. He, while they purify him, stands high over all things that exist Soma, a God as Surya is.

XVII Soma Pavamana

1. By generation long ago this God, engendered for the Gods,

Flows tawny to the straining cloth.

2. According to primeval plan this poet hath been strengthened by,

The sage as God for all the Gods.

3. Shedding the ancient fiuid thou art poured into the cleansing sieve:

Roaring, thou hast produced the Gods.

XVIII Soma Pavamana

1. Bring near us those who stand aloof: strike fear into our enemy:

O Pavamana, find us wealth!

2. To him the active, nobly born.

3. Sing ye your songs to him, O men!

XIX Soma Pavamana

1. The Somas skilled in song, the waves have led the water forward, like

Buffaloes speeding to the woods.

2. With stream of sacrifice the brown bright drops have flowed with strength in store

Of kine into the wooden vats.

3. To Indra, Vayu. Varuna to Vishnu and the Maruts let

The Soma juices flow expressed.

XX Soma Pavamana

1. O Soma, for the feast of Gods, river-like he hath swelled with surge,

Sweet with the liquor of the stalk, as one who wakes, into the vat that drops with meath.

2. Like a dear son how must be decked, the bright and shining one hath clad him in his robe.

Men skilful at their work drive him forth, like a car, into the rivers from their hands.

XXI Soma Pavamana

1. The rapture-shedding Somas have flowed forth in our assembly, pressed.

To glorify our liberal lords.

2. Now like a swan hemaketh all the company sing each his hymm

He like steed is bathed in milk.

3. And Trita's maidens onward urge the tawny-coloured with the stones,

Indu for Indra, for his drink.

XXII Soma Pavamana.

1. Herewith flow on, thou friend of Gods! Singing, thou runnest round the sieve oni every side.

The streams of meath have been effused.

2. Lovely, gold-coloured, on he flows.

3. For him who presses, of the juice.

BOOK II
CHAPTER I

I Soma Pavamana

1. Soma, as leader of the song, flow onward with thy wondrous aid.

For holy lore of every sort!

2. Do thou as leader of the song, stirring the waters of the sea,

Flow onward, known to all mankind!

1 O Soma, O thou Sage, these worlds stand ready to enhance thy might:

The milch-kine run for thy behoof.

II Soma Pavamana

1. Indu, flow on, a mighty juice; glorify us among the folk:

Drive all our enernies away!

2. And in thy friendship, Indu, most sublime and glorious, may we

Subdue all those who war with us!

3. Those awful weapons which thou hast, sharpened at point to strike men down--

Guard us therewith from every foe!

III Soma Pavamana

1. O Soma, thou art strong and bright, potent, O God, with potent sway,

2. Steer-strong thy might is like a steer's, steer-strong the wood, steer-strong the juice:

A steer indeed, O Steer, art thou.

3. Thou, Indu, as a vigorous horse, hast neighed together steeds and kine:
Unbar for us the doors to wealth!

IV Soma Pavamana

1. For thou art strong by splendour: we, O Pavamana call on thee,
The brilliant looker on the light.
2. When thou art sprinkled with the streams, thou reachest, purified by men,
Thy dwelling in the wooden vat.
3. Do thou, rejoicing, nobly-armed! pour upon us heroic strength.
O Indu, come thou hitherward!

V Soma Pavamana

1. We seek to win thy friendly love, even Pavamana's flowing o'er
The limit of the cleansing sieve.
2. With those same waves which in their stream o'erflow the purifying sieve,
Soma, be gracious unto us!
3. O Soma, being purified, bring us from all sides-for thou canst-
Riches and food with hero sons!

VI Agni

1. Agni we choose as envoy, skilled performer of this holy rite,
Hotar, possessor of all wealth.
2. With constant calls they invocate Agni, Agni, Lord of the house,
Oblation-bearer, much-beloved
3. Bring the Gods hither, Agni, born for him who trims the Sacred grass:
Thou art our Hotar, meet for praise!

VII Mitra Varuna

1. Mitra and Varuna we call to drink the draught of Soma juice,
Those born endowed with holy strength.
2. Those who by Law uphold the Law, Lords of the shining light of Law,
Mitra I call, and Varuna.
3. Let Varuna be our chief defence, let Mitra guard us with all aids,
Both make us rich exceedingly!

VIII Indra

1. Indra the singers with high praise, Indra reciters with their lauds,
Indra the choirs have glorified.
2. Indra is close to his two bays, with chariot ready at his word,
Indra the golden, thunder-armed.
3. Help us in battles Indra, in battles where thousand spoils are gained,
With awful aids, O awful one!
4. Indra raised up the son aloft in heaven, that he may see afar:
He burst the mountain for the kine.

IX Indra-Agni

1. To Indra and to Agni we bring reverence high and holy hymn,
And, craving help, soft words with prayer.
2. For all these holy singers thus implore these twain to succour them,
And priests that they may win them strength.
3. Eager to laud you, we with songs invoke you, bearing sacred food,
Fain for success in sacrifice.

X Soma Pavamana

1. Flow onward, mighty with thy stream, inspiriting the Marut's Lord,

Winning all riches with thy power!

2. I send thee forth to battle from the press, O Pavamana, strong,

Sustainer, looker on the light!

3. Acknowledged by this song of mine, flow, tawnycoloured, with thy stream:

Incite to battle thine ally!

XI Soma Pavamana

1. A Red Bull bellowing to the kine, thou goest, causing the heavens and earth to roar and thunder.

A shout is heard like Indra's in the battle: thou flowest on, sending this voice before thee.

2. Swelling with milk, abounding in sweet juices, urging the meathrich plant thou goest onward.

Making loud clamour, Soma Pavamana, thou flowest when thou art effused for Indra.

3. So flow thou on inspiriting, for rapture, turning the weapon of the water's holder!

Flow to us wearing thy resplendent colour, effused and eager for the kine. O Soma!

XII Indra

1. That we may win us wealth and power we poets verily, call on thee:

In war men call on thee, Indra, the hero's Lord, in the steed's race-course call on thee

2. As such, O wonderful, whose hand holds thunder, praised as mighty, Caster

of the Stone!

Pour on us boldly, Indra, kine and chariot-steeds, ever to be the conqueror's strength!

XIII Indra

1. To you will I sing Indra's praise who gives good gifts, as we I we know;

The praise of Maghavan who, rich in treasure, aids his singers with wealth thousandfold.

2. As with a hundred hosts, he rushes boldly on, and for the offerer slays his foes.

As from a mountain fiow the water-brooks, thus flow his gifts who feedeth many a one.

XIV Indra

1. O Thunderer, zealous worshippers gave thee drink this time yesterday:

So, Indra, listen here to him who offers lauds: come near unto our dwelling-place!

2. Lord of bay steeds, fair-helmed, rejoice thee: thee we seek. Here the disposers wait on thee.

Thy glories, meet for praise! are highest by the juice, O Indra, lover of the song.

XV Soma Pavamana

1. Flow onward with that juice of thine most excellent, that brings delight,

Slaying the wicked, dear to Gods!

2. Killing the foeman and his hate, and daily winning spoil and strength,

Gainer art thou of steeds and kine.

3. Red-hued, be blended with the milk that seems to yield its lovely breast,

Falcon-like resting in thine home!

XVI Soma Pavamana

1. As Pashan, Fortune, Bhaga, comes this Soma while they make him pure.

He, Lord of all the multitude, hath looked upon the earth and heaven.

2. The dear cows sang in joyful mood together to the gladdening drink.

The drops as they are purified, the Soma juices, make the paths.

3. O Pavamana, bring the juice, the mightiest, worthy to be famed,

Which the Five Tribes have over them, whereby we may win opulence!

XVII Soma Pavamana

1. Far-seeing Soma flows, the Steer, the Lord of hymns, the furtherer of days, of mornings, and of heaven.

Breath of the rivers, he hath roared into the jars, and with the help of sages entered Indra's heart.

2. On, with the sages, flows the poet on his way, and guided by the men, hath streamed into the vats.

He, showing Trita's name, hath caused the meath to flow, increasing Vayu's strength to make him Indra's friend.

3. He, being purified, hath made the mornings shine, and it is he who gave the rivers room to flow.

Making the three-times seven pour out the milky stream, Soma, the cheerer, yields whate'er the heart finds sweet.

XVIII Indra

1. For so thou art the brave man's friend; a hero, too, art thou, and strong:

So may thy heart be won us!

2. So hath the offering. wealthiest Lord, been paid by all the worshippers.

So dwell thou, Indra, even with us!

3. Be not thou like a slothful priest, O Lord of spoil and strength: rejoice

In the pressed Soma blent with milk!

XIX Indra

1. All sacred songs have magnified Indra expansive as the sea.

Best of all warriors borne on cars, the Lord of heroes, Lord of strength.

2. Lord of might, Indra, may we ne'er, strong in thy friendship, be afraid!

We glorify with praises thee, the never conquered conqueror.

3. The gifts of Indra from of old, his saving succours never fail,

When to his worshippers he gives the boon of booty rich in kine.

CHAPTER II

I Soma Pavamana

1. These rapid Soma-drops have been poured through the purifying sieve.

To bring us all felicities.

2. Dispelling manifold mishap, giving the courser's progeny,

Yea, and the warrior steed's, success.

3. Bringing prosperity to kine, they pour perpetual strengthening food

On us for noble eulogy.

II Soma Pavamana.

1. King Pavamana is implored with holy songs, on man's behalf,

To travel through, the realm of air.

2. Pressed for the banquet of the Gods, O Soma, bring us might,and speed,

Like beauty for a'brilliant show!

3. Bring us, O Indu, hundredfold increase of kine, and noble steeds.

The gift of fortune for our help!

III Soma Pavamana

1. With sacrifice we seek to thee fair cherisher of manly might

In mansons of the lofty heavens.

2. Drink gladdening, crusher of the bold, praiseworthy, with most mighty sway,

Destroyer of a hundred forts.

3. Hence riches came to thee, the King, O sapient one: the strong-winged bird,

Unwearied, brought thee from the sky.

4. And now, sent forth, he hath attained to mighty power and majesty,

Active and ready to assist.

5. That each may see the light, the bird brought us the guard of Law, the friend

O fall, the speeder through the air.

IV Soma Pavamana

1. For food, flow onward with thy stream, cleansed and made bright by sapient men:

Indu, with sheen approach the milk!

2. While thou art cleansed, song-lover. bring comfort and vigourto the folk,

Poured, tawny one! on milk and curds!

3. Purified for feast of Gods, go thou to Indra's resting-place,

Resplendent, furthered by the strong!

V Agni.

1. By Agni Agni is inflamed, Lord of the house, wise, young,. who bears

Our gifts: the ladle is his mouth.

2. God, Agni, be his sure defence who, lord of sacrificial gifts.

Worshippeth thee the messenger.

3. Be gracious, brilliant Godl to him who, rich in sacred gifts,would fain

Call Agni to the feast of Gods!

VI Mitra Varuna

1. Mitra of holy strength I call, and foe-destroying Varuna,

Who perfect prayer with offered oil.

2. By Law, O Mitra, Varuna, Law-strengtheners who cleave to Law,

Have ye obtained your lofty power.

3. The Sages, Mitra, Varuna, of wide dominion, mighty ones,

Bestow on us effectual strength.

VII Maruts

1. So mayst thou verily be seen coming with fearless Indra: both

Of equal splendour, bringing bliss!

2. Thereafter they, as is their wont, resumed the state of new-born babes,

Taking their sacrificial name.

3. Thou, Indra, with the rapid Gods who shatter even what is firm,

Even in the cave didst find the cows.

VIII Indra-Agni

1. I call the twain whose deed wrought here hath all been famed in ancient time:

Indra and Agni harm us not!

2. The strong, the scatterers of the foe, Indra and Agni we invoke:

May they be kind to one like me:

3. Ye slay our Arya foes, O Lords of heroes, slay our Dasa foes:

Ye drive all enemies away.

IX Soma Pavamana.

1. The living drops of Soma juice pour, as they flow the gladdening drink,

Intelligent drops above the station of the sea, exhilarating, dropping meath.

2. May Pavamana, King and God, speed with his wave over the sea the lofty rite!

Do thou by Mitra's and by Varuna's decree flow furthering the lofty rite:

3. Far-seeing, lovely, guided by the men, the God whose habitation is the sea!

X Soma Pavamana

1. Three are the voices that the car-steed utters: he speaks the lore of prayer, the thought of Order.

To the cows' master come the cows inquiring: the hymns with eager longing come to Soma.

2. To Soma come the cows, the milch-kine longing, to Soma sages with their hymns inquiring.

Soma, effused, is purified and lauded: our hymns and Trishtup songs unite in Soma.

3. Thus, Soma, as we pour thee into vessels, while thou art purified, flow for our welfare!

Pass into Indra. with great joy and rapture: make the voice swell, and generate abundance!

XI Indra

1. O Indra, if a hundred heavens and if a hundred earths were thine,--

No, not a hundred suns could match thee at thy birth, not both the worlds, O Thunderer.

2. Thou, hero, hast performed thy hero deeds with might, yea, all with strength, O strongest one.

Maghavan, help us to a stable full of kine, O Thunderer, with wondrous aids!

XII Indra

1. We compass thee like water, we whose grass is trimmed and Soma pressed.

Here where the filter pours its stream, thy worshippers round thee, O Vritra-slayer, sit.

2. Men, Vasu! by the Soma with lauds call thee to the foremost place.

When cometh he athirst unto the juice as home, O Indra, like a bellowing bull?

3. O valiant hero, boldly win thousandfold spoil with Kanva's sons!

O active Maghavan, with eager prayer we crave the yellowhued with store of kine.

XIII Indra

1. With Plenty for his true ally the active man will gain the spoil.

Your Indra, much-invoked, I bend with song, as bends a wright his wheel of solid wood.

2. They who bestow great riches love not paltry praise: wealth comes not to the niggard churl.

Light is the task to give, O Maghavan, to one like me on the decisive day.

XIV Soma Pavamana

1. Three several words are uttered: kine are lowing cows. who give the milk:

The tawny-hued goes bellowing on.

2. The young and sacred mothers of the holy rite have uttered praise,

Embellishing the Child of Heaven.

3. From every side, O Soma, for our profit, pour thou forth four seas.

Filled full of riches thousandfold!

XV Soma Pavamana

1. The Somas, very rich in sweets, for which the sieve is distined,

flow Effused, the source of Indra's joy: may you strong juices reach the Gods!

2. Indu flows on for Indra's sake,-thus have the deities declared.

The Lord of Speech exerts himself, controller of all power and might.

3. Inciter of the voice of song, with thousand streams the ocean flows.

Even Soma, Lord of opulence, the friend of Indra, day by day.

XVI Soma Pavamana

1. SPREAD is thy cleansing filter, Brahmanaspati: as prince thou enterest its limbs from every side.

The raw; whose mass bath not been heated. gains not this: they only which are dressed, which bear, attain to it.

2. High in the seat of heaven is placed the scorcher's sieve: its, threads are standing separate, glittering with light.

The swift ones favour him who purifieth this: with brilliancy they mount up to the height of heaven.

3. The foremost spotted Steer bath made the Mornings shine: he bellows, fain for war, among created things.

By his high wisdom have the mighty Sages wrought: the Fathers who behold mankind laid down the germ.

XVII Agni

1. Sing forth to him, the holy, most munificent, sublime with his refulgent glow,

To Agni, ye Upastutas

2. Worshipped with gifts, enkindled, splendid, Maghavan shall win

himself heroic fame:

And will not his more plentiful benevolence come to us with abundant strength?

XVIII Indra

1. We sing this strong and wild delight of thine which conquers in the fray,
Which, Caster of the Stone! gives room and shines like gold.
2. Wherewith thou foundest shining lights for Ayu and for Manu's sake:
Now joying in this sacred grass thou bearnest forth.
3. This day too singers of the hymn praise, as of old, this might of thine:
Win thou the waters every day, thralls of the strong!

XIX Indra

1. O Indra, hear Tirschi's call, the call of him who serveth thee.
Satisfy him with wealth of kine and valient offspring! Great art thou.
2. For he, O Indra, hath produced for thee the newest gladdening song,
A hymn that springs from careful drop thought, ancient and full of sacred truth.
3. That Indra will we laud whom songs and hymns of praise have magnified.
Striving to win, we celebrate his many deeds of hero might.

BOOK III
CHAPTER I

I Soma Pavamana

1. Fleet as swift steeds thy cows celestial have been poured, O Pavamana, with the milk into the vat.

Sages who make thee bright, O friend whom Rishis love, have shed continuous streams from out the realm of air.

2. The beams of Pavamana, sent from earth and heaven his ensigns who is ever stedfast, travel round.

When on the sieve the golden-hued is cleansed he rests within the jars as one who seats him in his place.

3. O thou who seest all things, sovran as thou art and passing strong, thy rays encompass every form.

Pervading with thy natural powers thou flowest on, and as the whole world's Lord, O Soma, thou art King.

II Soma Pavamana

1. From heaven hath Pavamana, made, as 'twere, the marvellous thunder, and

The lofty light of all mankind.

2. The gladdening and auspicious juice of thee, O Pavamana, King!

Flows o'cr the woollen straining-cloth.

3. Thy juice, O Pavamana, sends its rays abroad fixe splendid skill,

Like lustre, all heaven's light, to see.

III Soma Pavamana

1. Impetuous, bright, have they come forth, unwearied in their speed, like bulls,

Driving the black skin far away.

2. May we attain the bridge of bliss, leaving the bridge of woe behind:

The riteless Dasa may we quell!

3. The mighty Pavamana's roar is heard as 'twere the rush of rain

The lightning-Rashes move in heaven.

4. Indu, pour out abundant food with store of cattle and of gold,

Of heroes, Soma! and of steeds!

5. Flow onward, dear to all mankind fi full the mighty heaven and earth,

As Dawn, as Surya with his beams

6. On every side, O Soma, flow round us with thy protecting stream,

As Rasa flows around the world!

IV Soma Pavamana

1. Flow on, O thou of lofty thought, flow swift in thy beloved form,

Saying, I go where dwell the Gods.

2. Preparing what is unprepared, and bringing store of food to man,

Make thou the rain descend from heaven

3. Even here is he who, swift of course, hath with the river's wave Rowed down.

From heaven upon the straining cloth.

4. With might. producing glare, the juice enters the purifying sieve,

Far-seeing, sending forth its light.

5. Inviting him from far away, and even from near at hand, the juice

For Indra is poured forth as meath.

6. In union they have sung the hymn: with stones they urge the golden-hued,

Indu for Indra, for his drink.

V Soma Pavamana

1. The glittering maids send Sdra forth, the glorious sisters, closeallied,

Send Indu forth, their mighty Lord.

2. Pervade, O Pavamana, all our treasures with repeated light,

Pressed out, O God thyself, for Gods!

3. Pour on us, Pavamana! rain, as service and fair praise for Gods:

Pour forth unceasingly for food!

VI Agni

1. The watchful guardian of the people hath been born, Agni, the very strong, for fresh prosperity.

With oil upon his face. with high heaven-touching flame, he shineth splendidly, pure, for the Bharatas.

2. O Agni, the Angirasas discovered thee what time thou layest hidden, fleeing back from wood to wood.

Thou by attrition art produced as conquering might, and men, O Angiras, call thee the Son of Strength.

3. The men enkindle Agni in his threefold seat, ensign of sacrifice, the earliest bousehold-priest.

With Indra and the Gods together on the grass let the wise priest sit to complete the sacrifice!

VII Mitra-Varuna

1. This Soma hath been pressed for you, Low-strengtheners, Mitra, Varuna!
List, list ye here to this may call!
2. Both Kings who never injure aught have come to their sublimest home,
The thousand-pillared, firmly based.
3. Worshipped with fat libation. Lords of gifts, Adityas, sovran Kings,
They wait on him whose life is true.

VIII Indra

1. Armed with the bones of dead Dadhyach, Indra with unresisted. might
The nine-and-ninety Vritras slew.
2. He, searching for the horse's head that in the mountains lay concealed,
Found it in Saryandvdn lake.
3. Then straight they recognized the mystic name of the creative Steer.
There in the mansion of the Moon.

IX Indra Agni

I. As rain from out the cloud, for you, Indra and Agni, from my thought
This noblest praise hath been produced.
2. Indra and Agni, listen to the singer's call: accept his songs.
Fulfil, ye mighty Lords, his prayers!
3. Give us not up to indigence, ye heroes, Indra, Agni, nor
To Slander and reproach of men!

X Soma Pavamana

1. Gold-Hued! as one who giveth strength flow on for Gods to drink, a draught

For Vayu and the Marut host!

2. The Steer shines brightly with the Gods, dear Sage in his appointed home.

Even Pavamana unbeguiled.

3. O Pavamana, sent by prayer, roaring about thy dwelling-place,

Ascend to Vayu as Law bids!

XI Soma Pavamana

1. O Soma, Indu, every day thy friendship hath been my delight.

Many fiends follow me; help me, thou tawny-hued: pass on beyond these barriers!

2. Close to thy bosom am I. Soma, day and night draining the milk, O golden hued.

Surya himself refulgent with his glow have we, as birds, o'ertaken in his course.

XII Soma Pavamana

1. Active, while being purified, he hath assailed all enemies: They deck the Sage with holy hymns.

2. The Red hath mounted to his shrine; strong Indra hath approached the juice:

In his firm dwelling let him rest!

3. O Indu, Soma, send us now great opulence from every side:

Pour on us treasures thousandfold!

CHAPTER II

I Soma Pavamana

1. Winner of gold and gear and cattle flow thou on, set as impregner, Indu! 'mid the worlds of life!

Rich in brave men art thou, Soma, who winnest all: these holy singers wait upon thee with song.

2. O Soma, thou beholdest men from every side: O Pavamana, Steer, thou wanderest through these.

Pour out upon us wealth in treasure and in gold: may we have strength to live among the things that be!

3. Thou passest to these worlds as sovran Lord thereof, O Indu, harnessing thy tawny well-winged mares.

May they pour forth for thee milk and oil rich in sweets:

O Soma, let the folk abide in thy decree!

II Soma Pavamana

1. The streams of Pavamana, thine, finder of all I have been ettused,

Even as Surya's rays of light.

2. Making the light that shines from heaven thou flowest on to every form,

Soma, thou swellest like a sea.

3. Shown forth thou sendest out thy voice, O Pavamana, with a roar.

Like Surya, God, as Law commands.

III Soma Pavamana

1. Hitherward have the Somas streamed, the drops while they are purified:

When blent, in waters they are raised.

2. The milk hath run to meet them like floods rushing down a precipice:

They come to Indra, being cleansed.

3. O Soma Pavamana, thou flowest as Indra's gladdener: The men have seized and lead thee forth.

4. Thou, Indu, when, expressed by stones, thou runnest to the filter, art

Ready for Indra's high decree.

5. Victorious, to be hailed with joy, O Soma, flow delighting men,

As the supporter of mankind!

6. Flow on, best Vritra-slayer; flow meet to be hailed with joyful lauds,

pure, purifying, wonderful

7. Pure, purifying, is he called, Soma effused and full of sweets,

Slayer of sinners, dear to Gods.

IV Soma Pavamana

1. The Sage hath robed him in the sheep's wool for the banquet of the Gods,

Subduing all our enemies.

2. For he, as Pavamana, sends thousandfold riches in the shape

Of cattle to the worshippers.

3. Thou graspest all things with thy mind, and purifiest thee with thoughts:

As such, O Soma, find us fame!

4. Pour on us lofty glory, send sure riches to our liberal lords:

Bring food to those who sing thy praise!

5. As thou art cleansed, O wondrous steed, O Soma, thou hast entered, like

A pious king, into the songs,

6. He, Soma, like a courser in the floods invincible, made bright

With hands, is resting in the press.

7. Disporting, like a liberal chief, thou goest. Soma to the sieve,

Lending the laud heroic strength.

V Soma Pavamana

1. Pour on us with thy juice all kinds of corn, each sort of nourishment!

And, Soma, all felicities!

2. As thine, O Indu, is the praise, and thine what springeth from, the juice,

Seat thee on the dear sacred grass!

3. And, finding for us steeds and kine, O Soma, with thy juice flow on

Through days that fly most rapidly!

4. As one who conquers, ne'er subdued, attacks and slays the enemy,

Thus, vanquisher of thousands! flow!

VI Soma Pavamana

1. Thou, Indu, with thy streams that drop sweet juices, which were poured for help,

Hast settled in the cleansing sieve.

2. So flow thou onward through the fleece, for Indra flow to be his drink,

Seating thee in the shrine of Law!

3. As giving room and freedom, as most sweet, pour butter forth and milk,

O Soma, for the Angirasas!

VII Agni

1. Thy glories are, like lightnings from the rainy cloud, visible, Agni, like the comings of the Dawns,

When, loosed to wander over plants and forest trees, thou crammest by thyself thy food into thy mouth.

2. When, sped and urged by wind, thou spreadest thee abroad, soon piercing through thy food according to thy will,

The hosts, who ne'er decayest, eager to consume, like men on chariots, Agni! strive on every side.

3. Agni, the Hotar-priest who fills the assembly full, waker of wisdom, chief controller of the thought-

Thee, yea, none other than thyself, doth man elect priest of the holy offering, great and small, alike.

VIII Mitra-Varuna

1. Even far and wide, O Varuna and Mitra, doth your help extend:

May I obtain your kind good-will!

2. True Gods, may we completely gain food and a dwelling place from you:

Ye Mitras, may we be your own!

3. Guard us, ye Mitras, with your guards, save us, ye skilled to save: may we

Subdue the Dasyus by ourselves!

IX Indra

I. Arising in thy might, thy jaws thou shookest Indra, having drunk

The Soma which the press had shed.

2. Indra, both world gave place to thee as thou wast fighting, when thou wast

The slayer of the Dasyu hosts.

3. From Indra, have I measured out a song eight-footed with nine parts,

Delicate, strengthening the Law.

X Indra-Agni

1. Indra and Agni, these our songs of praise have sounded forth to you:

Ye who bring blessings! drink the juice

2. Come, Indra, Agni, with those teams, desired of many, which ye have,

O heroes, for the worshipper

3. With those to his libation poured, ye heroes, Indra, Agni, come:

Come ye to drink the Soma-juice!

XI Soma Pavamana

1. Soma, flow on exceeding bright with loud roar to the reservoirs,

Resting in wooden vats thy home!

2. Let water winning Somas flow to Indra, Vayu, Varuna,

To Vishnu and Marut host!

3. Soma, bestowing food upon our progeny, from every side

Pour on us riches thousandfold.

XII Soma Pavamana

1. Pressed out by pressers Soma goes over the fleecy backs of sheep,

Goes even as with a mare in tawny-coloured stream, goes in a sweetly-sounding stream.

2. Down to the water Soma, rich in kine, bath flowed with cows, with cows that have been milked.

They have approached the mixing-vessels as a sea: the cheerer streams for the carouse.

9 789360 075880

Printed at Repro India Ltd.